THE WRITINGS OF
J. M. SYNGE

ROBIN SKELTON

THE BOBBS-MERRILL COMPANY, INC.

INDIANAPOLIS · NEW YORK

The Bobbs-Merrill Company, Inc.
Indianapolis · New York

Copyright © 1971 by Robin Skelton

All Rights Reserved

Library of Congress Catalog card number
LC72–142488

Printed in Great Britain

THE WRITINGS OF J. M. SYNGE

CONTENTS

INTRODUCTION

In writing this book I have tried to take into account the uses to which it will be put and the existence of other books on the same subject. I have therefore avoided extensive comment on matters which have been thoroughly discussed elsewhere, while indicating in an appendix the places where those discussions can be found. I have kept biographical data to the minimum necessary to establish Synge's approach to his own work, in the belief that those in search of biographical information will read the biography by David H. Greene and Edward M. Stephens (Collier Books, 1961). I have attempted to make each chapter a separate entity in the belief, well supported by experience, that students are likely to read individual chapters of immediate concern to them rather than read the whole book. This means that I have permitted myself a certain amount of repetition of key points. I have quoted other writers on Synge only when it seemed really necessary to do so, and never in order to indulge in that form of one-sided debate which has little function but to reveal that the author has read the relevant books in the field. I would rather be faulted for my own opinions than praised for manipulating those of others. It has been said that a scholarly book can be defined as one in which the apparatus dwarfs the subject matter. If such be the case, this book is not scholarly. I have kept footnotes to the minimum, and have seen no reason to quarrel publicly with those who hold different opinions.

Although the opinions given here are, as I have said, my own, they have been formed as a consequence of reading a great many books, a number of which I have listed in an appendix.

Almost all of these works were written without their authors having had the opportunity to examine Synge's unpublished manuscripts and notebooks. Thus none of these books deals with *When the Moon Has Set*, the verse plays, and the autobiographical notes, or refers to the early drafts of the familiar plays. The publication of the Oxford University Press edition of the Collected Works of J. M. Synge has now provided us all with texts of everything that anyone could possibly need to read, and also with many details of early drafts of the plays, poems, and prose works, together with many passages from Synge's notebooks and letters. I have used this edition of Synge throughout my book and, except where I have indicated otherwise, every quotation from Synge is taken from it. The references in brackets at the close of each quotation are to the relevant volume and page of that edition. Though myself the General Editor of that work, I cannot claim to be responsible for more than its first volume. The Plays edited by Ann Saddlemyer, and the Prose, edited by Alan Price, testify to their scholarship and not to mine. I must, therefore, express my gratitude to them for labours which have made this present book possible, and emphasize that the many differences between the previously accepted texts and those of the Oxford edition make this edition the only one upon which it is safe to base critical judgments of the work of J. M. Synge.

To my expressions of gratitude to Dr Saddlemyer, Dr Price, and Oxford University Press for their work, and for permission to utilize their discoveries, I must add my thanks to Mrs Lilo Stephens and the Synge Estate for making all this material available for study and publication.

Some parts of this book have already been published in slightly different versions. The chapter on *The Shadow of the Glen* appeared in *English* in October 1969. The chapter on *Riders to the Sea* first appeared as part of my Introduction to an edition of the Houghton Library version of *Riders to the Sea* published by the Dolmen Press in 1969. The chapter on the poems is based upon an essay published in *Poetry Ireland* in 1962.

R. S.

The University of Victoria,
British Columbia

CHAPTER ONE

Early Work

The early work of any author is likely to be of more biographical than literary interest and in looking it over it is as well to keep in mind the circumstances in which it was written. J. M. Synge was born on 16 April 1871 at Rathfarnham near Dublin. His father died in 1872, and the boy was brought up by his mother, a woman of firm religious convictions. There were three elder children in the family. Shortly after the death of her husband Mrs Synge moved house to 4 Orwell Park, Rathgar, next door to her mother, and it was here that J. M. Synge lived until he became a student at Trinity College. The summer holidays were spent at Greystones in County Wicklow, where Mrs Synge rented a house for the required period. Synge's first writings were made in collaboration with his cousin, Florence Ross, with whom he used to explore the woods surrounding Rathfarnham Castle, studying ornithology and collecting birds' eggs. These took the form of a nature diary. Florence was the first girl to interest him emotionally.

His interest in nature persisted into his late adolescence. He joined the Dublin Naturalists' Field Club (founded in 1886) and remained a member until 1888, though he wrote no papers for it. In some autobiographical notes he made later in Paris, he described two spiritual crises. The first occurred in early childhood.

I was painfully timid, and while still very young the idea of Hell took a fearful hold on me. One night I thought I was irretrievably damned and cried myself to sleep in vain yet terrified efforts to form a conception of eternal pain. In the morning I renewed my lamentations and my mother was sent for. She comforted me with the assurance that the Holy Ghost was convicting me of sin and thus preparing me for ultimate salvation. This was a new idea, and I rather approved. (II. 4)

The second was caused by reading Charles Darwin.

When I was about fourteen I obtained a book of Darwin's. It opened in my hands at a passage where he asks how can we explain the similarity between a man's hand and a bird's or bat's wings except by evolution. I flung the book aside and rushed out into the open air – it was summer and we were in the country – the sky seemed to have lost its blue and the grass its green. I lay down and writhed in an agony of doubt. My studies showed me the force of what I read, [and] the more I put it from me the more it rushed back with new instances and power. Till then I had never doubted and never conceived that a sane and wise man or boy could doubt. I had of course heard of atheists but as vague monsters that I was unable to realize. It seemed that I was become in a moment the playfellow of Judas. Incest and parricide were but a consequence of the idea that possessed me. My memory does not record how I returned home nor how long my misery lasted. I know only that I got the book out of the house as soon as possible and kept it out of sight, saying to myself logically enough that I was not yet sufficiently advanced in science to weigh his arguments, so I would do better to reserve his work for future study. In a few weeks or so I regained my composure, but this was the beginning. Soon afterwards I turned my attention to works of Christian evidence, reading them at first with pleasure, soon with doubt, and at last in some cases with derision. (II. 10)

By the time he was 'sixteen or seventeen', he tells us in these autobiographical fragments, he had 'renounced Christianity'. Indeed, for a while he 'renounced everything' and then made himself 'a sort of incredulous belief that illuminated nature and lent an object to life without hampering the intellect'.

This story is easily told, but it was a terrible experience. By it I laid a chasm between my present and my past and between myself and my kindred and friends. Till I was twenty-three I never met or at least knew a man or woman who shared my opinions. (II. 11)

Synge was not only alienated from his family by his disbelief, but also by his political sympathies. For the most part he avoided argument, though he objected, in 1885, to his brother Edward's eviction of tenants in Cavan, Mayo, and Wicklow; his mother, however, felt these activities to be correct and moral.

When he was sixteen he began to study music, and took violin lessons. Later he became a student at the Royal Irish Academy of music. A year after graduating from Trinity

College, Dublin, where he had studied Gaelic and taken considerable interest in Irish antiquities, he visited Germany and
there he wrote several poems of a little more interest than the
few he had composed as an adolescent. He also made his first
fumbling attempts at sketching ideas for plays. Most of his work
of this period relates directly to his experiences and particularly
to the confusions and tensions provided by several unsatisfactory
love affairs. One in particular distressed him. Although Cherry
Matheson was very fond of him, she could not agree to marry a
non-believer. His convictions deprived his desires of satisfaction;
the intellect opposed the heart.

In 1894 he renounced music and turned to literature. *Vita
Vecchia*, written in 1895-7, consisted of a series of poems linked
together by a prose narrative, describing the supposed circumstances which occasioned the verse. The verse itself is, in its
original versions, melodramatically full of despair and introspec-
tion, and thick with crude alliteration, and the narrative is a
perfunctorily disguised version of his affair with Cherry Matheson. Archaisms and inversions abound. There are unfortunate
epithets. One poem refers to 'pearly eyes', a phrase which
unintentionally suggests blindness; another begins 'Sweet
seemeth it'. Nevertheless, in one poem passion breaks through.
An early version of it is headed, 'My lady left me and I said'. It
reads:

> I curse my bearing, childhood, youth
> I curse the sea, sun, mountains, moon,
> I curse my learning, search for truth,
> I curse the dawning, night and noon.
>
> Cold, joyless I will live, though clean,
> Nor, by my marriage, mould to earth
> Young lives to see what I have seen,
> To curse – as I have cursed – their birth.   (II. 19)

The curse upon 'learning' and 'search for truth' while obviously
referring to his difficulties with Cherry Matheson, also anticipates some of the attitudes of the later prose and drama. The
piece ends with a series of general reflections which were
completed in 1907 when Synge revised the work. One of these
reads:

We do wrong to seek a foundation for ecstasy in philosophy or the hidden things of the spirit – if there is spirit – for when life is at its simplest, with nothing beyond or before it, the mystery is greater than we can endure.

(II. 24)

Afterthought though it may be, this passage is similar in feeling to several written in 1896–8 in the autobiographical notes. In these it is the power of nature which is described.

In my childhood the presence of furze bushes and rocks and flooded streams and strange mountain fogs and sunshine gave me a strange sense of enchantment and delight but I think when I [rested] on a mountain I sat quite as gladly looking on the face of a boulder as at the finest view of glen and river.

(II. 12)

In another place he wrote:

I think the consciousness of beauty is awakened in persons as in peoples by a prolonged unsatisfied desire. . . . Perhaps the modern feeling for the beauty of nature as a particular quality – an expression of divine ecstasy rather than a mere decoration of the world – arose when men began to look on everything about them with the unsatisfied longing which has its proper analogue in puberty. . . . The feeling of primitive people is still everywhere the feeling of the child; an adoration that has never learned or wished to admire its divinity. This feeling everyone will recognize in Wordsworth's *Ode*, though he does not seem perhaps to give it its truest interpretation. (II. 13)

The Wordsworthian element in Synge's appreciation of nature must not be underestimated. Wordsworth was his first enthusiasm in poetry. In his autobiographical notes he wrote:

One evening when I was collecting on the brow of a long valley in County Wicklow wreaths of white mist began to rise from the narrow bogs beside the river. Before it was quite dark I looked round the edge of the field and saw two immense luminous eyes looking at me from the base of the valley. I dropped my net and caught hold of a gate in front of me. Behind the eyes there rose a black sinister forehead. I was fascinated. For a moment the eyes seemed to consume my personality, then the whole valley became filled with a pageant of movement and colour, and the opposite hillside covered itself with ancient doorways and spires and high turrets. I did not know where or when I was existing. At last someone spoke in the lane behind me – it was a man going home – and I came back to myself. The night had become quite dark and the eyes were no longer visible, yet I recognized in a moment what had caused the apparition – two clearings in a wood lined with white mist divided again by a few trees which formed the eye-balls. For many days afterwards I could not look on these fields even in daylight without terror. (II. 10)

This passage is a 1907 revision of earlier material, but the sentence which follows it was written in 1898:

It would not be easy to find a better instance of the origin of local super-stitions, which have their origin not in some trivial accident of colour but in the fearful and genuine hypnotic influence such things possess upon the prepared personality. (II. 10)

The personality of Synge was, by 1898, almost fully prepared to respond to experience in this imaginative fashion. He had felt the agony of belief and the agony of doubt. He had seen how religious conviction may lead to emotional deprivation and des-pair, and noted how the morality of bourgeois Protestantism can accept and praise cruelty and social brutality. He had grown to believe that simplicity and intuition could lead to ecstasy more directly than philosophy. Alienated from his family and his early environment he had experienced the effects of solitude; and, having studied both Gaelic and Irish antiquities he was ready to join, as he did join, the Nationalist movement. Though his membership of the Irish League lasted only for a few months of 1897, he had, by the time he came to visit Aran, become once more keenly interested in Celtic culture.

It was in 1897 that he wrote his essay 'Under Ether' in which he described his impressions of being anaesthetized and operated on for the removal of swollen glands in his neck in December 1897. The essay is his first extended attempt at describing the world of dream and reverie. While just about to succumb he 'yelled with fury' at the doctors: 'I'm an initiated mystic. I could rend the groundwork of your souls.' A dream followed:

I seemed to traverse whole epochs of desolation and bliss. All secrets open before me, and simple as the universe to its God. Now and then something recalled my physical life, and I smiled at what seemed a moment of sickly infancy. At other times I felt I might return to earth, and laughed aloud to think what a god I should be among men. For there could be no more terror in my life. I was a light, a joy. (II. 42)

Awakening from the dream and unable wholly to recall its details he thought:

If I could only remember I'd write books upon books; I'd teach all earth of delight. (II. 43)

Then, when fully awake:

I took notice of every familiar occurrence as if it were something I had come back to from a distant country. The impression was very strong on me that I had died the preceding day and come to life again, and this impression has never changed. (II. 43)

In this essay Synge first touched on that sense of being unable entirely to remember and yet being equally unable to forget ancient spiritual knowledge, which suffuses passages of *The Aran Islands*.

In 1899 Sygne wrote another autobiographical work, which he called *Étude Morbide* and later condemned. It takes the form of a diary written by a violinist preparing to give a recital. His mistress, the Cellianini, is encouraging, but he grows ever more nervous. He takes a new pupil, Mlle Chouska, who appears to him to be the exact complement of the Cellianini. He writes 'The first is like an oak or fir tree, the other some vague growth of the sea' (II. 26). The recital is a failure and the Cellianini is led from the concert room in hysterics and deposited in a lunatic asylum, where she dies. The violinist, harrowed by morbid thoughts, contemplates suicide but reads Chouska's copy of the *Imitation of Christ*, which drives all thoughts of suicide away. For a time he nurtures himself 'in a more than saintly exaltation' (II. 30) but soon comes to think his 'religious ecstasy' may be a 'morbid growth' (II. 32). He reads Spinoza and goes to Brittany where he lives with the peasants and plays his fiddle for them, becoming interested in stories of the supernatural. On returning to Paris he falls in love with the Chouska but they decide finally that marriage would spoil what has been a spiritual love. He abandons poetry and drama as well as music, and says 'I will be silent' (II. 36). The last letter he receives from the Chouska concludes: 'In the end we will dream away our existences, happier than in the world' (II. 36). This obviously owes a great deal to Synge's own experiences. It utilizes his doubts of his own musical abilities, his meditations upon religious truth, his appreciation of peasant life in Brittany, as well as his difficulties with his girl friends.

It also clearly reveals many of the problems he was finding it necessary to solve as regards his approach to artistic creation, and there are many passages which shed light upon his obsessions of the time.

All living things demand their share of joy, and I see no permanent joy apart from the creation or touching of beautiful forms or ideas. This is the immortal fragment of religion. As art may decorate what is useful or exist for its own beauty in itself, so an action done with a beautiful motive is decorated and joyful, and for souls that are barred from the joy of activity there is still the quiescent ecstasy of resignation. (II. 31)

I am hearing many ghost stories. Since I have come back to nature my rather crude materialism has begun to dissatisfy me. Nature is miraculous and my own dreams were something extra-human. (II. 33)

I am yielding up my imagination to the marvellous. These things cannot be understood without an intimate if cautious sympathy, and I long to lift the veil and to see with my own inward sight the pretended symbols of the soul. (II. 34)

I have come out among the hills to write music again if I am able. . . . All art that is not conceived by a soul in harmony with some mood of the earth is without value, and unless we are able to produce a myth more beautiful than nature – holding in itself a spiritual grace beyond and through the earthly – it is better to be silent. . . . When I am here I do not think without a shudder of the books of Baudelaire or Huysmans. Among heather I experience things that are divine, yet I know not how I should express them. Music is the finest art, for it alone can express directly what is not utterable, but I am not fitted to be a composer. To-day I burned many sonnets written in Paris with an ecstasy of pride, for they were but a playing with words and I blushed to bear them before the solemnity of God. . . . There is little poetry that I can read here, except the songs of the peasants and some of Wordsworth and Dante. . . . (II. 35)

While the conclusion of *Étude Morbide*, with its decadent rejection of reality for dream, may remind us more of Villiers de l'Isle Adam than of the author of the *Playboy*, and while many of the diary entries seem to be demanded by the nature of the fiction, the above paragraphs so closely resemble attitudes of mind which we find in *The Aran Islands* that we must accept them as being approximations to Synge's own views.

Clearly, while Synge remained anti-clerical he did not remain materialist. In many of his works he shows sympathy with the near-mystical view that art must be 'in harmony with some mood of the earth', and that he yielded up his imagination to the marvellous can scarcely be denied by any reader of *The Well of the Saints* or *The Aran Islands*.

Étude Morbide was first drafted in 1899, as I have said. Synge, who was thrifty with his manuscripts, revised it after a time, probably in 1907, though he never seems to have considered publishing it, any more than he considered publishing *Vita Vecchia*, though this too he first revised and then quarried for poems which could be reshaped for his book of *Poems and Translations* (1909).

It seems that the vast majority of Synge's central themes were in his mind before the turn of the century. The conflict between reason and emotion which runs through all the plays and finds its most explicit expression in *The Well of the Saints* and the *Playboy*, the love of simplicity and distrust of philosophy which is shown in the Aran book, and the love of the marvellous, of 'wonders', are all to be found in these early pages. Moreover, in these works written before and during the composition of the notes which later made up *The Aran Islands* there is an element of fictionalized autobiography and a concentration upon the innermost feelings and reveries of the protagonist rather than upon objective factual description. All the characters in *Vita Vecchia* and *Étude Morbide* derive their significance from being part of the narrator's emotional and spiritual explorations. The conflicts are not between opposed characters but opposed or counterpointing sensations. Everything is in the mind of the narrator who is, in his approach to reality, and for all his religious doubts, a good deal nearer mysticism than materialism.

CHAPTER TWO

When the Moon Has Set

On 12 December 1907 Synge wrote to Leon Brodsky: 'I wrote one play – which I have never published – in Paris, dealing with Ireland of course, but not a peasant play, before I wrote *Riders to the Sea*' (III. 155). Although this seems categorical enough, *When the Moon Has Set* did not in fact reach the form in which Synge finally left it until 1903, after *Riders to the Sea* had been completed and read to Yeats and Lady Gregory. It appears to have begun in 1896–8 with some notes and snatches of dialogue, to have been worked on and added to in 1898 and 1899, and to have been completed as a two-act drama some time between 1900 and September 1901, when it was read by Yeats and Lady Gregory and rejected by them as a possibility for an Abbey Theatre production. 'It was after its rejection by us he took to peasant work,' Yeats wrote in a memorandum concerning it in 1909.

The rejection, however, seems to have led Synge to rework the play rather than abandon it, and in his diary for 23 May 1903 he wrote: 'Finished (?) one act Play "When the Moon Has Set (?)" ' In fact it looks as if the play was further revised before being abandoned, though Synge thought enough of it to leave it among his papers as something to be considered by his executors.

The plot of the final version is simple. Colm Sweeney, a young man, returns from a country walk to the house where his uncle has just died and tells the maid, Bride, of having met a madwoman. Bride tells him that it was Mary Costello, whose portrait as a young woman hangs over the fireplace of the room in which they are talking. Sister Eileen, the young nun who has been looking after the dying man, returns to the house and tells Colm that his uncle once wished to marry Mary Costello, 'but when it was all arranged she broke it off because he did not believe in God' (III. 165), and later went mad. Colm tries to make Sister Eileen realize that 'in evading her impulses this woman did what was wrong and brought this misery on my uncle and herself' (III. 165). He attempts to persuade her to abandon her order and 'obey the earth' (III. 169). Their argument is interrupted by the entry of Mary Costello who, after much raving about her solitude and the children she has never had, says to the two young people:

God save you kindly the two of you. There's great marrying in the world but it's late we were surely, and let yourselves not be the same. Let you mind the words I was saying, and give no heed to the priests or the bishops of the angels of God, for it's little the like of them, I was saying, knows about women or the seven sorrows of the earth.   (III. 173)

Colm takes up the argument with Sister Eileen again when Mary Costello has left, and she exchanges her nun's habit for a green dress, and the play ends with the following exchange:

SISTER EILEEN: I have left my veil in the room where your uncle is lying. . . . I seem to be in a dream that is wider than I am. I hope God will forgive me. I cannot help it.
COLM: How many people ask to be forgiven for the most divine instant of their lives. Let us be wiser than they are. *He takes up one of the rings.* Here is the ring that was the sorrowful heirloom of my uncle. Give me your hand. I, the male power, have overcome with worship you, the soul of credulous feeling, the reader of the saints. From our harmonized discord new notes will rise. In the end we will assimilate with each other and grow senseless and old. We have incarnated God, and been a part of the world. That is enough. *He takes her hand.* In the name of the Summer, and the Sun, and the Whole World, I wed you as my wife. *He puts the ring on her finger.*   (III. 177)

The last sentence alone would explain why Yeats and Lady Gregory thought the play unsuitable. It would have caused a riot. The play is also unsatisfactory in other respects. The characterization is poor. Colm is too obviously a vehicle for the author's opinions and Sister Eileen is little more than cardboard. Mary Costello is more fully realized, and her speeches have a vividness and power that reminds one of Synge's mature drama. This is not very surprising as her part was not created until 1902. The play is dependent for its tension almost entirely upon argument, and its suspense is very much of the 'Will she or won't she?' variety. It is, indeed, a bad play, and clearly originated in Synge's wish somehow to exorcize the memory of Cherry Mathcson's intransigence. If he could not persuade her in actuality, he would at least convince her simulacrum in a drama.

There would be very little point in discussing this play at all were it not that in its early drafts it contains speeches which show Synge attempting to develop a philosophy of life, and gathering together in this one work a large quantity of earlier ideas and theories. The 1901 version indicates that the hero, now called Columb, was once a musician and he receives a letter from Paris in which there are passages from both *Vita Vecchia* and *Étude Morbide*. In an earlier fragment there are also passages from the autobiographical notes.

Many of the passages which were intended to present philosophical truth are confused, over-emotional, and sloppy in terminology. Nevertheless they indicate Synge's struggle towards that certainty of stance which gives his mature drama its authority and perceptiveness.

An early piece of dialogue (1896–8) reads:

All emotions have neither end nor beginning, they are part of a long sequence of impulse and effect. The only relative unity in art is that of a whole man's lifetime. Hamlet though seeming complete is but the link from Romeo and Lear, as Shakespeare is the link from Chaucer to Byron, and modern literature from classical to what we are approaching. . . .   (III. 278)

This reveals yet again Synge's impulse towards discovering unity in all things. The kind of unity he discovered is shown in a note of 1898:

Every life is a symphony and the translation of this sequence into music and from music again, for those who are not musicians, into literature, or painting or sculpture, is the real effort of the artist.   (III. 279)

This sentence is used in its entirety in the completed two-act version of the play. It occurs in a manuscript of Columb's which

Eileen reads aloud, and is followed by a revision of the passage about emotions quoted above:

The emotions which pass through us have neither end nor beginning, are a part of eternal sensations, and it is this almost cosmic element in the person which gives all personal art a share in the dignity of the world.   (III. 174)

The phrase 'personal art' is significant. Synge clearly still felt, in 1901, that if a human being were to present his emotional reactions to experience he would be presenting something of more true significance than if he were to record objective fact. It is our emotions which link us with the cosmos and not our reasoning power. This, surely, is one theme of *The Aran Islands*, and it appears also in *The Shadow of the Glen*, *The Tinker's Wedding*, and *The Well of the Saints*, where we are made to applaud the reasons of the heart rather than those of the head or the social conventions. There is another version of these passages in a manuscript of 1898 which emphasizes for us this personal element in art:

Every life is a symphony, and the translation of this life into music, and from music back to literature or sculpture or painting is the real effort of the artist. The emotions which pass through us have neither end nor beginning – are a part of the sequence of existence – and as the laws of the world are in harmony it is this almost cosmic element in the person which gives great art, as that of Michelangelo or Beethoven, the dignity of nature.

   I do not think biography – even autobiography – can give this revelation. But while the thoughts and deeds of a lifetime are impersonal and concrete – might have been done by anyone – art is the expression of the essential or abstract beauty of the person.   (II. 3)

This passage is reminiscent of one in *Étude Morbide* where the diarist tells us:

For a week I have nurtured myself in a more than saintly exultation. I am forming from my own spirit a divine and beautiful existence and I am as much an artist in my peculiar precincts as Beethoven or Wagner. . . . (II. 30)

The point is driven home at the end of the 1901 *When the Moon Has Set*. Columb soliloquizes:

Every life is a symphony. It is this cosmic element in the person which gives all personal art, and all sincere life, and all passionate love a share in the dignity of the world . . . If art is the expression of the abstract beauty of the

person there are times when the person is the expression of the beauty that is beyond the world. . . . (III. 174)

It is the 'personal art' we admire in the lyrical outbursts of Synge's dreamers and fantasists. It is 'sincere life' that we admire in the rebellious Sarah Casey, and the love-starved Nora Burke. It is passionate love which is the dream of Pegeen Mike and the fatal destiny of Deirdre of the Sorrows.

So far there is nothing that runs counter to Christianity, unless we regard Christianity as inevitably involving the repression of emotional life. *When the Moon Has Set* does suggest this, and the hero is filled with fear of death arriving before life has received its emotional dues. In the 1901 version he says:

There is an anguish in this splendour of June. One feels one's mortality. . . . The furze bushes are withering already, and the hawthorn is decayed. (III. 164)

His next speech runs:

It is natural for old men to die. This pageant of blossoms that fades in a few hours is far more terrible. Don't you realize the irony of beautiful life? Diamonds and rubies that do not feel are beautiful for ever, but women and flowers fulfil their task of propagation and wither in a day. It is sadder than death. (III. 164)

Later still he restates the theme with greater intensity:

Death is always terrible. . . . The last few nights – I suppose because I am not strong – I have been haunted by that appalling sensation in which we realize the gulf of annihilation we are being whirled into. . . . (III. 164)

Christian belief might, one would think, have brought him comfort, but he derides Christianity because it has failed. He refers to the 'stagnation of belief'. The world he sees as 'an orchestra where every living thing plays one entry and then gives his place to another. We must', he tells Eileen, 'be careful to play all the notes' (III. 176). The true players have left Christianity:

The people who rebel from the law of God are not those who are essaying strange notes in the dark alleys of the world but the fools who linger in the aisles droning their withered chants with senile intonation. (III. 176)

He says 'In the Christian synthesis each separate faculty has been dying of atrophy. The synthesis has fallen,' and he tells her

that the imagination has now wandered away alone to grow powerful again until men 'will grow human again with a more wonderful manhood. Every passion will unite in new discords resolving in what are to us inconceivable harmonies' (III. 176).

This is less anti-Christian than anti-clerical. Colm's vision of life does not exclude, but emphasizes, an element of the Divine.

The only calm of importance is the calm of the man who feels the vortex of passion and death straining beneath him and is able to deride it. . . . The world is a mode of the Divine exaltation and every sane fragment of force ends in a fertile passion that is filled with joy. It is the infertile excitements that are filled with death. That is the whole moral and aesthetic of the world.
(III. 168)

This passage from a draft of the 1901 version anticipates one theme of *The Shadow of the Glen*, and provides a philosophical justification of Synge's worship of the exuberant, for to deny life its vitality is to deny a central truth. Colm says:

The worst vice is slight compared with the guiltiness of a man or woman who defies the central order of the world. . . . The only truth a wave knows is that it is going to break. The only truth a bud knows is that it is going to expand and flower. The only truth we know is that we are a flood of magnificent life the fruit of some frenzy of the earth. . . . The European races may be swept away, humanity itself may die out, but a turmoil of life is within us. It has come from eternity and I suppose it will go on for eternity. (III. 168)

In *When the Moon Has Set* Synge constructed, upon the foundations he had laid in his autobiographical notes, and in *Vita Vecchia* and *Étude Morbide*, a structure of beliefs and attitudes which provided him with perspectives he utilized in his later prose, drama and poetry. His view of the 'eternal' and 'cosmic' significance of human emotions enabled him to create prose works in which subjective feeling dominates factual reportage, and plays in which passion is elevated above reason. His view of the symphonic and musical nature of experience permitted him to experiment with a highly rhythmic language and with dramatic structures that are free of the constrictions which vitiate much conventional drama of his time. His anti-clericalism he managed to combine with something approaching nature mysticism so that, while conventional Christian attitudes and shibboleths could be derided, the spiritual element in man could

22

still be emphasized and praised. It is perhaps ironic that the final version of *When the Moon Has Set* is less interesting than fragments of earlier drafts, and that Synge's first completed play should end up as a simple one-act morality based upon the thesis that frustration of the emotions leads to insanity and asceticism fails in reverence for life, although its earlier drafts contain so much discussion of more profound matters. Begun before his first visit to Aran, continued during the years in which the Aran notes formed themselves into a book, and completed only after the prose work was finished, its various drafts serve as a commentary upon Synge's views during this crucial period of his growth as a writer.

CHAPTER THREE

The Aran Islands

W. B. Yeats claimed the credit for directing Synge's attention to the Aran Islands. In his introduction to *The Well of the Saints* he described meeting Synge in Paris and saying to him: 'Give up Paris. You will never create anything by reading Racine, and Arthur Symons will always be a better critic of French literature. Go to the Aran Islands. Live there as if you were one of the people themselves; express a life that has never found expression' (III. 63).

According to Synge's diary the two men first met on 21 December 1896. Yeats had been to Aran during the summer and he told John O'Leary in a letter that his imagination was 'full of those grey islands', a phrase he incorporated later in his introduction to *The Well of the Saints*.

Yeats' accounts of his life and contacts are rarely to be accepted as unvarnished truth. Wisdom after the event was often permitted to colour his recollections. His advice to Synge, to 'express a life that has never found expression', therefore may reasonably be regarded as much as a comment upon what Synge did as an accurate memory of what he told Synge to do.

Synge first visited Aran from 10 May to 25 June 1898. He spent two weeks on Inishmore (Aranmor), and four on Inishmaan. He returned in the summers of 1899, 1900, 1901 and 1902. He spent, in all, a total of four and a half months on the islands.

During his stay he filled many pages of his notebooks with impressions and anecdotes. These notes he revised with considerable care and severity, and in 1901 at Yeats' suggestion he offered the finished manuscript to Grant Richards, who thought the book of limited interest and rejected it. It was finally published by Elkin Mathews in association with Maunsel and Company in 1907.

It is always dangerous to guess at the influences which affect a writer's approach to a given piece of writing, but in the case of *The Aran Islands* we are on safer ground than usual. In 1897, after his meeting with Yeats, Synge read several of Yeats' books, *The Wanderings of Oisin, The Countess Kathleen and Various Legends and Lyrics, The Land of Heart's Desire, The Secret Rose*, and *The Celtic Twilight*. He also read Paulam's *Nouveau Mysticisme* and some of the *Proceedings* of the Society of Psychical Research. The inclusion of these last two in his reading list shows that his reawakened interest in things Irish had been augmented by a more general interest in the supernatural.

In April of 1897 he heard a lecture on Brittany by the folklorist Anatole le Braz. This sent him to le Braz's own works, *Au Pays des Pardons, Vielles Histoires du Pays Breton, La Légende de la Mort chez les Bretons Armoricaines*. He also read other books about Brittany and in 1898, not long before visiting Aran, he read Pierre Loti's *Pêcheur d'Islande*, a copy of which he took with him on his trip. These books all to a greater or lesser extent emphasized the importance of preserving what remained of Celtic customs. Synge was especially impressed by Pierre Loti whose concern was less with the scholarly than with the picturesque and dramatic. In one draft of his Introduction to *The Aran Islands* Synge wrote: 'The general plan of this book is, it will be seen at once, largely borrowed from Pierre Loti, who has, I think, treated this sort of subject more adequately than any other writer of the present day' (II. 48). This sentence he later cancelled, for his view of Pierre Loti changed, and in another suppressed passage, after castigating Emily Lawless for the ignorance of peasant life which she showed in her Aran novel, *Grania* (1892), he wrote, 'Miss Lawless if she has erred has not done so as deeply as Pierre Loti in his *Pêcheur d'Islande*' (II. 103).

To these bookish influences we may tentatively add another. The first Protestant missonary to the Aran Islands was Synge's uncle, the Rev. Alexander Synge. He arrived there in 1851 and disliked what he saw. He described himself as 'surrounded by dirt and ignorance', and was, perhaps understandably, inclined to 'attack' 'the bad ways, religion, etc.' of the people. He told his brother in a letter how he had succeeded in 'putting a stop to a ball match that used to go [on] here every Sunday'. Later he bought a motor-boat and started commercial fishing in competition with his parishioners, thinking it necessary to arm his crew in case of opposition.[1]

Synge's view of his 'pious relations' was such as to make his certain knowledge of his uncle's career an added incentive to glorify the pagan wildness of the islanders. It is worth noting that there are two references to the Rev. Alexander Synge in *The Aran Islands*. The first is made early in the first part.

This evening an old man came to see me, and said he had known a relative of mine who passed some time on this island forty-three years ago.

'I was standing under the pier-wall mending nets,' he said, 'when you came off the steamer, and I said to myself in that moment, if there is a man of the name of Synge left walking the world, it is that man yonder will be he.'

(II. 53)

The second reference is made in the third part of the book. An old man tells Synge that 'when he first left the island as a cabin-boy, between forty and fifty years ago' (II. 147), he visited Dublin, and, while walking on the quay, was with his companions invited to Mr Synge's house, because they were all from Aran.

Mr Synge brought us into his kitchen and gave the men a glass of whisky all round, and a half-glass to me because I was a boy – though at that time and to this day I can drink as much as two men and not be the worse of it. We were some time in the kitchen, then one of the men said we should be going. I said it would not be right to go without saying a word to Mr Synge. Then the servant-girl went up and brought him down, and he gave us another glass of whisky, and he gave me a book in Irish because I was going to sea, and I was able to read in the Irish.

I owe it to Mr Synge and that book that when I came back here, after not hearing a word of Irish for thirty years, I had as good Irish, or maybe better Irish, than any person on the island. (II. 47)

One may guess that Synge took some pleasure in showing his reverend uncle dispensing whisky and Gaelic to the islanders he had made uncomfortable during his missionary period, and that he relished the clear implication that of all his uncle's actions this was the only one that remained in the memory of Aran.

In suggesting this I am, perhaps, allowing fancy to qualify fact. It is, however, noticeable that Synge's view of Aran is that of a partisan, not of the Protestant bourgeois ethic, but of the 'primitive' sensibility of the islanders. He records one man telling a story of the supernatural and referring to a character in the tale as 'one of them Protestants who don't believe in any of these things and do be making fun of us'. He wrote in a suppressed passage words which he probably thought too argumentative to include in an ostensibly non-polemical book:

The thought that this island will gradually yield to the ruthlessness of 'progress' is as the certainty that decaying age is moving always nearer the cheeks it is your ecstasy to kiss. How much of Ireland was formerly like this and how much of Ireland is today Anglicized and civilized and brutalized. . . . Am I not leaving in Inishmaan spiritual treasure unexplored whose presence is as a great magnet to my soul? In this ocean alone is not every symbol of the cosmos? (II. 103)

The Aran Islands was not intended to be an objective book. Nor was it intended to be a tourists' guide. Synge does not discuss the architecture of the churches, and is incurious about the exact nature of the 'Duns, or pagan forts'. Daniel Corkery tells us that:

Partisans in later years questioned the islanders about him, and were glad to learn that he spent most of his days lying alone in the sun or, equally alone, moping around under the stars!
. . . They discovered also that he did not frequent the really authoritative people on the islands who could have told him everything about everything. He preferred the happy-go-lucky folks who were not authorities on anything: the simple ones were friends of his; blind men and callow youths he would spend long hours with; he preferred rambling stories that had not a word of truth in them to the pronouncements of the wise.[2]

Corkery goes on to say that Synge's book is better than most books written 'by people who had never dreamt of linking themselves into the life of the region they dealt with', and praises the work for its deep insight into the 'consciousness of the people'. He also sees it as valuable for the insight it gives us into 'Synge's own consciousness, his fundamentally emotional nature', and finds it important for its provision of 'the raw material on which

the dramatist was afterwards to try his creative powers'. Corkery's view is the general one, and yet, when one looks further
into the matter it may seem somewhat superficial.

Synge himself, intentionally or unintentionally, laid a number
of false trails. In his Introduction he suggested that the book was
no more than a simple account of his experiences.

In the pages that follow I have given a direct account of my life on the
islands, and of what I met with among them, inventing nothing, and chang-
ing nothing that is essential. (II. 47)

The word 'essential' begs a question or two. In writing to
Spenser Brodney in 1907, after saying that it was in making *The
Aran Islands* and in writing about 'the Wicklow peasantry' that
he learned to write 'the peasant dialect and dialogue' he used in
his drama, he said '*The Aran Islands* throws a good deal of light
on my plays' (II. 47). If this last statement refers only to the
stories and descriptions which are later used in his drama, the
words 'sheds a good deal of light' seem, to me at least, a little
overemphatic. What 'light' other than that illuminating the
origin of plot, and image, and word-play does *The Aran Islands*
shed?

Perhaps the best way to approach this problem is to start with
the realization that, though *The Aran Islands* may have been used
to provide material for plays, it was not originally written
as a source book only, though Synge may well have had
this function in mind. Secondly, having dutifully noted possible
influences, it might be as well to forget all about them and look,
not at the origins of the book, but the book itself, realizing that
in order to view it as an aesthetic creation it might also be
advisable to ignore its role (given it largely by other and later
writers) in the nationalist movement of its time. Thirdly,
because a book purporting to be a description of actuality is
likely to blind the reader to both its defects and its excellences by
persuading him that the former are inevitable failures inherent
in the nature of the source material and the latter simply 'direct
accounts' of providential happenings, let us pretend that *The
Aran Islands* is completely fiction, and read it as we read *Erewhon*,
or *News from Nowhere*, or *Gulliver's Travels*, noting the way in

which it presents value-systems at variance with the established ones of so-called 'civilization'.

The Aran Islands is told in the first person, and, like *Étude Morbide*, is in journal form. It consists of four sections, each devoted to one visit to the area. The narrator is a sensitive man receptive to beauty, and easily impressed by the grotesque and the vivid. The opening pages of the first section (II. 49–51) present, like an overture, the various themes which go to make up the whole. The mysterious isolation of the island is shown by the way in which its shoreline, at first visible, is then lost in mist, and then reappears as 'a dreary rock'. It is as if a veil between one world and the next has been pierced. The second theme, that of the humble nature of Aran society, and the simplicity of the islanders' lives, is introduced with an image of the narrator's fellow passengers, the girls with their heads twisted in shawls, and the 'young pigs tied loosely in sacking'.

The theme of desolation, allied to the theme of constant awareness of death, is then introduced. The narrator tells us 'I have seen nothing so desolate', and adds that on his walk:

Occasionally I passed a lonely chapel or schoolhouse, or a line of stone pillars with crosses above them and inscriptions asking a prayer for the soul of the person they commemorated.   (II. 49)

This mood of desolation, however, is broken into by an awareness of humour and vitality, as the narrator meets a group of girls who hurry past him 'with eager laughter and great talking in Gaelic'.

The theme of untidy confusion, of careless muddle, then emerges as we are told of the broken panes of the public-house and the pigs playing untended in the surf.

It is only after all these observations on the part of the narrator that we hear another voice, and an old man talks of antiquarians who have visited the islands, and tells the first of many stories which reveal the islanders' strong belief in the supernatural and their conviction of the superiority of their stories 'over all other stories in the world'. The first movement of the book then ends with a little girl mending the turf fire, and a reference to their being many grown women who 'have never set a foot upon the mainland'. Thus the theme of the islands' solitude is repeated, and we are, indeed, returned to the first sentence of the whole book in which the narrator describes himself as 'sitting over a turf fire' recalling his voyage and his arrival.

These are the main themes, expressed here simply and easily, and with a rhythmic recurrence that is characteristic of the shape of the whole book as well as of the prose style. The narrator is not the protagonist of the work, in that he is largely only receptive to impressions, and only occasionally stimulates activity or event. These occasions, however, increase in number as the book grows until in the fourth section we find him playing his fiddle for the islanders' dance, and, having now learned Gaelic, involving himself in conversation and story to a greater extent than previously. Passive appreciation gives place to active involvement, though not to the origination of activities. Moreover, as the book develops, the narrator's feelings about the islands intensify, and his language becomes more vivid and more assured. The book itself, also, becomes more fragmentary and the narrative less connected, as if the narrator no longer found it necessary to explain his emotions to himself, but had grown to accept his insight as being, of necessity, fragmentary and occasional. The book thus shows, as far as the developing character of the narrator goes, a movement from a rather low-key meditative coherence to a much more vivid fragmentation. At the beginning it seems that all details are recorded; the narrator is uncertain as to which will prove of importance and therefore puts all down in his recollections. Towards the end he displays decisiveness, and rejects some of the material offered him, as being of no real significance.

The Aran Islands is not, however, the self-portrait of its narrator; the narrator is used to show the way in which the islands impress themselves upon a receptive sensibility and give its owner an understanding of a system of values alien to all his previous experience, and a perspective upon the nature of cultural inheritance.

The theme of cultural inheritance is introduced first in a reference to those antiquarians who had visited the islands before

Synge. The old blind man refers to 'Petrie and Sir William Wilde' among others. He then tells a story of the faerie, thus presenting another aspect of the islands' cultural heritage. The narrator visits beehive huts, but does not describe them at all adequately. He tells us:

When we crawled in on our hands and knees, and stood up in the gloom of the interior, old Mourteen took a freak of earthy humour and began telling what he would have done if he could have come in there when he was a young man and a young girl along with him.

Then he sat down in the middle of the floor and began to recite old Irish poetry, with an exquisite purity of intonation that brought tears to my eyes though I understood but little of the meaning.

On our way home he gave me the Catholic theory of the fairies.   (II. 54–5)

It is this passage which first indicates the narrator's particular interest in the islands. He is not concerned with the stony remnants of the remote past; he is more interested in the way in which the beliefs and attitudes of the past are now mingled with those of more recent origin, and in the fusion of pagan and ancient attitudes with Christian ones. He tells us that on the islands 'the life is perhaps the most primitive that is left in Europe' (II. 53), and then, throughout the book, amasses evidence that this primitive society is, because of its intimate awareness of ancient things, and because of its retention of old beliefs, in some ways more truly civilized or, in one sense of the word, 'cultured' than the society of more advanced places.

When Mourteen tells him that Diarmid 'was killed by the druids, who put a burning shirt on him' (II. 57) he recalls the story of Hercules, and is half inclined to believe that the similarity is due to the retention of ancient beliefs rather than to a garbled memory of teachings by hedge schoolmasters. He speaks of the way in which the islanders' implements have each 'almost a personal character' which gives the life 'something of the artistic beauty of medieval life' (II. 58–59). When he is told the story of O'Connor, he comments:

The incident of the faithful wife takes us beyond Cymbeline to the sunshine on the Arno, and the gay company who went out to Florence to tell narratives of love. It takes us again to the low vineyards of Würzburg on the Main, where the same tale was told in the Middle Ages, of the 'Two Merchants and the Faithful Wife of Ruprecht von Würzburg'.

The other portion dealing with the pound of flesh, has a still wider distribution, reaching from Persia and Egypt to the *Gesta Romanorum*, and the *Pecorone* of Ser Giovanni, a Florentine notary. (II. 65)

The O'Connor story was first published as 'A Story from Inishmaan' in the *New Ireland Review*, and the narrator then finished by saying:

It is hard to assert at what date such stories as these reached the west. There is little doubt that our heroic tales which show so often their kinship with Grecian myths, date from the pre-ethnic period of the Aryans, and it is easy to believe that some purely secular narratives share their antiquity. Further, a comparison of all the versions will show that we have here one of the rudest and therefore, it may be, most ancient settings of the material. (II. 65)

Such a vast generalization would have been out of place in *The Aran Islands*, for it would have replaced the gradual cumulation of impressions and fragmentary speculations with a thesis, and thus altered the whole nature of the book. The point is, however, made clearly enough as the book proceeds. Stories heard, and events observed, on the islands are related to Breton folklore, Oriental music, and experiences of German and Polish people, and many stories, though told without commentary, are close enough to familiar folk-tales and myths of other lands to make the point without benefit of comment. The strange ramshackle 'Ballad of the White Horse' given in Part Four brings this theme to a climax. It refers to Adam, Babylon, Nebuchadnezzar, Noah, Moses, Pharaoh, Saul, David, Judas Maccabeus, Cyrus, Troy, Job, Hannibal Scipio, Brian Boru, Patrick Sarsfield, James II, Daniel O'Connell. The story is simple. The white horse has been present at, or taken part in, most of the great events of history, and has served many great men. He has now returned to Erin and is 'ready once more for the field'. The old man who gave the narrator the ballad hoped that he would print it:

. . . for it would not be fair, he says, that it should die out of the world, and he is the only man here who knows it, and none of them have ever heard it on the mainland. (II. 171)

The two other poems the old man tells, 'Rucard Mor' and

'Phelim and the Eagle', are less wide-ranging in allusion, but quite as obviously archetypal and mythic.

It is not only by means of allusions and echoes that the universal and primitive nature of the Aran culture is presented. The narrator frequently interprets what he observes in these terms. Thus he says of the men of the 'south island':

These strange men with receding foreheads, high cheek-bones, and ungovernable eyes seem to represent some old type found on these few acres at the extreme border of Europe, where it is only in wild jests and laughter that they can express their loneliness and desolation. (II. 140)

Later, talking of the men of Inishmaan, he refers to their being 'moved by strange archaic sympathies with the world' (II. 142). He uses the words 'pagan' and 'primitive' to describe the life of the islands with great frequency, but sees these qualities as enhancing rather than limiting the sensibility of the people. He talks of 'the singularly spiritual expression that is so marked in one type of the West Ireland women', and adds:

Later in the day, as the old man talked continually of the fairies and the women they have taken, it seemed that there was a possible link between the wild mythology that is accepted on the islands and the strange beauty of the women. (II. 54)

Half accepting the truth of these stories, he finds on Inishmaan that he is 'forced to believe in a sympathy between man and nature', and later talks of the 'supernatural beauty that comes over the island so often in rainy weather'.

The islanders are, however, not only spiritual, in touch with ancient beliefs and memories, and moved intimately by the powers of nature; they are also passionately aware of their isolation and of mortality. Speaking of the keen over the grave of an old woman the narrator tells us:

The grief of the keen is no personal complaint for the death of one woman over eighty years, but seems to contain the whole passionate rage that lurks somewhere in every native of the island. In this cry of pain the inner consciousness of the people seems to lay itself bare for an instant, and to reveal the mood of beings who feel their isolation in the face of a universe that wars on them with winds and seas. They are usually silent, but in the presence of death all outward show of indifference or patience is forgotten, and they

33

shriek with pitiable despair before the horror of the fate to which they are all doomed. (II. 75)

He sees this despair as a universal lament of man, and in another place shows the intensity of this feeling in an unforgettable image. A young man has died and the men digging the grave are obliged to break up a coffin:

... that was in the place into which the new one had to be lowered. When a number of blackened boards and pieces of bone had been thrown up with the clay, a skull was lifted out, and placed upon a gravestone. Immediately the old woman, the mother of the dead man, took it up in her hands, and carried it away by herself. Then she sat down and put it in her lap – it was the skull of her own mother – and began keening and shrieking over it with the wildest lamentation.

As the pile of mouldering clay got higher beside the grave a heavy smell began to rise from it, and the men hurried with their work, measuring the hole repeatedly with the two rods of bramble. When it was nearly deep enough the old woman got up and came back to the coffin, and began to beat on it, holding the skull in her left hand. This last moment of grief was the most terrible of all. The young women were nearly lying among the stones, worn out with their passion of grief, yet raising themselves every few minutes to beat with magnificent gestures on the boards of the coffin. The young men were worn out also, and their voices cracked continually in the wail of the keen. (II. 161)

The intensity of the islanders' feelings is increasingly shared by the narrator. Early in the first part he talks of the 'exquisite satisfaction' he feels in 'moving away from civilization' in a curagh (II. 57). A little later his expressions intensify:

No-one who has not lived for weeks among these grey clouds and seas can realise the joy with which the eye rests on the red dresses of the women, especially when a number of them are to be found together. (II. 67)

His own vision becomes mythic.

I noticed one extraordinary girl in the throng who seemed to exert an authority on all who came near her. Her curiously formed nostrils and narrow chin gave her a witch-like expression, yet the beauty of her hair and skin made her singularly attractive. (II. 68)

Later still he talks of poteen which 'brings a shock of joy to the blood' (II. 73). Watching the gulls he feels that he can 'understand the greater part of their cries', and says:

There is one plaintive note which they take up in the middle of their usual

34

babble with extraordinary effect, and pass on from one to another along the cliff with a sort of an inarticulate wail, as if they remembered for an instant the horror of the mist. (II. 74)

He sees the jumble of horses being loaded on to a ship in terms of 'a mass of struggling creatures' (II. 79). He has a dream which he describes in phrases of extreme intensity: 'terrible agony', 'ecstasy', 'uncontrollable frenzy' (II. 100). His feelings on other occasions are described as 'indescribably acute'. He grows 'flushed with exultation' and, talking of the islanders in the second part of the book, he says:

There is hardly an hour I am with them that I do not feel the shock of some inconceivable idea, and then again the shock of some vague emotion that is familiar to them and to me. (II. 113)

Watching a girl he finds that:

At one moment she is a simple peasant, at another she seems to be looking out at the world with a sense of prehistoric disillusion and to sum up in the expression of her grey-blue eyes the whole external despondency of the clouds and sea. (II. 114)

The narrator's involvement in his own interpretations is such that the whole book becomes much less the account of a series of visits to strange islands than an account of an introspective myth-making which feeds upon any evidence that supports it. The myth itself only forms gradually, and is brought to completion by the outpouring of the three final ramshackle poems that combine wildness of imagination with half recollected learning and an intuitive feeling for heroic values which are now decayed and mutilated as the consequence of isolation.

The islanders, then, have virtues which are not of civilization. Though intensely passionate they are also reserved except at moments of grief and pain when they are proud of betraying excessive emotion. When young, the women are beautiful, filled with awareness of universal myth and natural forces, and, when old, figures of terrible power and decision. An old woman talks of her son as 'the first ruffian in the whole big world', and the narrator comments:

On these islands the women live only for their children, and it is hard to estimate the power of the impulse that made this old woman stand out and curse her son. (II. 92)

Another old woman, being evicted, bursts out with wild imprecations.

She belonged to one of the most primitive families on the island, and she shook with uncontrollable fury as she saw the strange armed men who spoke a language she could not understand driving her from the hearth she had brooded on for thirty years. (II. 89)

The picture of the old woman brooding 'for thirty years' is heroic; 'uncontrollable fury' is a phrase appropriate to the savagery of epic.

The furniture and implements of the islanders are described as:

. . . full of individuality, and being made from materials that are common here, yet to some extent peculiar to the island, they seem to exist as a natural link between the people and the world that is about them. (II. 59)

Here the word 'seem' establishes the narrator as the sensibility through which these matters are interpreted and transfigured. It is a word frequently used. In claiming aristocracy for these peasants he says:

Their way of life has never been acted on by anything much more artificial than the nests and burrows of the creatures that live round them, and they *seem* in a certain sense to approach more nearly to the finer type of our aristocracies – who are bred artificially to a natural ideal – than to the labourer or citizen, as the wild horse resembles the thoroughbred rather than the hack or cart-horse. (II. 66)

The men, we are told, 'feel *in a certain sense* the distinction of their island' (II. 77). Meeting Michael in Galway, the narrator is struck with 'the refinement of his nature', and notes that though the beach was 'crowded with half-naked women' neither Michael nor his friend '*seemed* to be aware of their presence' (II. 105). An old woman recited a poem 'with exquisite musical intonation, putting a wistfulness and passion into her voice that *seemed* to give it all the cadences that are sought in the profoundest poetry' (II. 112). On the train going east from Galway to Dublin on the eighth anniversary of Parnell's death the narrator tells us that:

The whole spirit of the west of Ireland, with its strange wildness and reserve, *seemed* moving in this single train to pay a last homage to the dead statesman of the east. (II. 124)

The use of the verb to seem and of the phrase 'in a certain sense' in these passages emphasizes the subjective nature of this book. It hints that while the narrator may appear to grow more and more intensely aware of the island's nature, and more able to take part in the society of which he was once only an observer, in reality he may be simply establishing for himself a personal myth which makes sense of his disturbed feelings on facing this environment. One cannot separate the dancer from the dance.

One can, however, having surveyed the myth-making, look at its implications. There is the story of the Connaught man who killed his father and who was given sanctuary by the islanders and saved from the law. The narrator tells us:

This impulse to protect the criminal is universal in the west. It seems partly due to the association between justice and the hated English jurisdiction, but more directly to the primitive feelings of these people, who are never criminals yet always capable of crime, that a man will not do wrong unless he is under the influence of a passion which is as irrepressible as a storm on the sea. If a man has killed his father, and is already sick and broken with remorse, they can see no reason why he should be dragged away and killed by the law.

Such a man, they say, will be quiet all the rest of his life, and if you suggest that punishment is needed as an example, they ask 'Would anyone kill his father if he was able to help it?' (II. 95)

After this portrayal of a natural moral sense more humane and civilized than that of other places, the narrator comments:

Some time ago, before the introduction of the police, all the people of the islands were as innocent as the people here remain to this day. . . . (II. 95)

He adds a little later:

It seems absurd to apply the same laws to these people and to the criminal classes of a city. (II. 96)

and describes how in these parts litigation leads to feuds and further violence. He tells us that evidence is never reliable on the islands, for:

37

. . . they think the claim of kinship more sacred than the claims of abstract truth. (II. 96)

'One law for the lion and ox is oppression,' said William Blake. It was Blake also who saw that reliance upon the reason may outlaw spiritual perception. Our narrator takes the same line:

. . . miracles must abound wherever the new conception of law is not understood. On these islands alone miracles enough happen every year to equip a divine emissary. Rye is turned into oats, storms are raised to keep evictors from the shore, cows that are isolated on lonely rocks bring forth calves, and other things of the same kind are common.

The wonder is a rare expected event, like the thunderstorm or the rainbow, except that it is a little rarer and more wonderful. Often, when I am walking and get into conversation with some of the people, and tell them that I have received a paper from Dublin, they ask me –

'And is there any great wonder in the world at this time?' (II. 128–9)

'Grandeur', 'distinction', 'individuality', 'innocence', 'wildness', 'passion', 'despair', are a few of the words most frequently used to describe the islanders. The smallest events are given extravagant dignity and beauty. We see the islands as a fallen paradise, where all the ancient knowledge, innocence and dignity remain, though sometimes in vestigial condition, and where awareness of a lost understanding of the powers of nature and super nature, gives the approach to death a more than usual intensity. The myths of the islanders are now garbled, but show in their fusion of Christian and pagan themes a half recollection of the all-embracing truth which unifies all story. The mist which separates Aran from the mainland is a barrier between the world of commonplace materialist life and the last remaining outpost of the life of the spirit in Europe.

Though the narrator gives us facts, quotes letters, and supports his creation with local references to places that we feel to have actuality, his language betrays the true subjective nature of his exploration. He discovers, finally, a world in which the opposing forces of ignorance and spiritual perceptiveness, passion and reticence, individualism and social tradition, love of life and fascination with death, exist in a harmony made more vivid by the people's conviction of their 'distinction' and their isolation from the 'world'. *The Aran Islands* is not a character study of its narrator; it is a pursuit of a vision of fallen man trapped halfway between earth and heaven. It shows how man will satisfy spiritual and emotional needs by transforming reality and selecting food for his imagination. It shows too how the creative imagination may, from peasants, rock and desolation, create a myth of startling intensity and power.

If we admit that by now we have abandoned the pretence that *The Aran Islands* has nothing to do with Synge's personal experiences on Aran, and return to the usual approach, it becomes clear just what Synge may have meant when he talked of the book shedding light on his plays. It is the value-system created in this book that gives us an indication of the attitude we must have in reading the later drama. In Inishmaan he found 'spiritual treasure' and this treasure remained 'a magnet' to his soul. He found in the Aran Islands that 'every symbol' was 'of the cosmos' (II. 103), in that the whole pattern of man as spirit, as animal, as social being, was there displayed in images as timeless and fundamental as those of universal myth.

The Aran Islands is not, however, a Utopian dream. It is not a *News from Nowhere*. Nor is it a satire, like *Erewhon* or *Gulliver's Travels*. It is closer to *Travels in Arabia Deserta* or even Lawrence's *Seven Pillars of Wisdom* in that, while purporting to be a plain account of places and people and events, it is in reality a poetic and philosophical interpretation of essential aspects of human life. It owes much to le Braz and Loti, but it also owes much to the dream-impregnated stories of Maeterlinck, one of whose books he took on his first visit to the islands. It is time, however, to remember that Synge had also been told to go to Aran by Yeats, whose own version of the Irish awareness of the supernatural, and of the forces of nature, was given in those books which Synge read in 1897. In *The Land of Heart's Desire*, Father Hart tells Mary and Maurteen of the fairies:

> Colleen, they are the children of the Fiend,
> And they have power until the end of time,
> When God shall fight with them a great pitched battle
> And hack them into pieces.[3]

In *The Aran Islands* 'old Mourteen' tells Synge 'the Catholic theory of the fairies':

When Lucifer saw himself in the glass he thought himself equal with God. Then the Lord threw him out of Heaven, and all the angels that belonged to him. While He was 'chucking them out' an archangel asked Him to spare some of them, and those that were falling are in the air still, and have power to wreck ships, and to work evil in the world.   (II. 56)

The similarity of 'Maurteen' and 'old Mourteen' is hard to accept as mere coincidence, especially as Synge admits to inventing names for his Aran characters. There are, understandably, other places where tales of the supernatural in *The Aran Islands* remind one of some in Yeats. It may be, indeed, that Synge in *The Aran Islands* was aware that in responding to Yeats' suggestion to go West, he had a necessity to make his own vision, and to oppose it to the dreaminess of Yeats. Certainly, Synge's passionate and vigorous version of the twilight (and the twilight, and the dark night itself frequently figure in *The Aran Islands*) contrasts with that of Yeats. *The Aran Islands* may be, indeed, the first time Synge, determined to be his own man, countered the Yeatsian vision with one more rudely passionate and virile.

Whether or not this is the case, *The Aran Islands* is, like Yeats' *The Celtic Twilight*, not merely an attempt to report upon the persistence of ancient culture and beliefs among the Irish peasantry, but a construction of images and values which have validity in themselves, and which point towards the importance of reviving, and maintaining, a particular sensibility in order to make sense of the predicament of humanity. If *The Aran Islands* is the rock upon which Synge's œuvre is founded, it is not the rock of newly recovered fact but that of fact transformed by the imagination into a vision of universal significance and creative utility.

CHAPTER FOUR

Riders to the Sea

On 20 January 1903 J. M. Synge visited W. B. Yeats and *Riders to the Sea* was read aloud by Lady Gregory in her rooms in London, and met 'with much approval', according to Synge's own diary entry. He was 'Chez Yeats' again the following morning, and it seems likely that, at this or a later meeting, Yeats suggested that the play should be published. It was read again in Yeats' rooms on 2 February, and a week later once more at Lady Gregory's when Arthur Symons heard it. He wrote to Lady Gregory the following morning to ask if 'Mr Sing would like to publish his play in the Fortnightly'. On 12 February Synge recorded in his diary that he had received a letter from Yeats' friend Arthur Symons 'asking my play for Fortnightly'. The play was sent off to Symons on 14 February, and on 16 February Synge wrote in his diary: 'Heard from Symons that my play is sent to Fortnightly.' On 10 March there is an entry, 'Got Riders to the Sea back from Fortnightly.' Synge was not much of a diarist. He never wrote down his feelings, or elaborated his plans. In the case of *Riders to the Sea* this is particularly irritating, because we know nothing further about it of any importance until the text is printed in *Samhain* of September–October 1903. On 18 December John Masefield wrote to Synge and asked him to send him a fair copy of the two plays, *The Shadow of the Glen* and *Riders to the Sea*, so that he might show them to Elkin Mathews, whom he had already tried to interest in *The Aran Islands*. The first performance of *Riders to the Sea* took place on 25 February 1904 in the Molesworth Hall. After many delays it was published, together with *The Shadow of the Glen*, in one volume of the Vigo Cabinet series, by Elkin Mathews, in 1905.

Riders to the Sea has, like many works of art, suffered somewhat from its popularity and from the activities of those critics who, faced with anything relating to the Irish peasantry, turn immediately into pseudo-sociologists, philologists, and Irish patriots. It is as absurd to regard this play as a work of merely regionalist interest as it would be to regard *Cymbeline* as a study of Roman Britain. Great drama escapes its locale and its time. Nevertheless, in reading the play those who have any knowledge at all of Irish drama will be forced to recall an earlier play by W. B. Yeats in which there are certain parallels to Synge's play. *Cathleen ni Houlihan* was first produced by W. G. Fay's Irish National Dramatic Company at St Teresa's Hall, Clarendon Street, Dublin, in 1902 on 2, 3, and 4 April. The lyrics from it were published in *The United Irishman* on 15 April. The play itself was published in *Samhain*, and as a book in October of the same year.

Synge's earliest notes for *Riders to the Sea* cannot be dated with any certainty. His first extended attempt at the play, however, has been dated by Dr Saddlemyer as belonging to the period spring–summer 1902. It seems, therefore, that Synge was writing *Riders to the Sea* with *Cathleen ni Houlihan* fresh in his mind.

The parallels between the two plays are not excessive, but they are interesting. Both plays are set in a cottage; both plays begin with a question; the protagonists in both plays introduce the main action by an examination of clothing; the old woman in both plays devotes much time to a rhetorical catalogue of the deaths of men attached to her; the young man whose immediate fate is the first concern of the play is in both cases called Michael; both plays end with the re-examination of the clothing involved.

These would be trivial parallels were it not that they were accompanied by mathematically precise contrasts. Yeats' Michael prepares for a wedding, and Synge's Michael for a funeral. Yeats' young men run down to the sea to join the French; Synge's Bartley goes down to the sea to travel to a horse-fair. The last words of Yeats' old woman imply a kind of immortality for the dead, for she sings:

They shall be remembered for ever,
They shall be alive for ever,
They shall be speaking for ever.
The people shall hear them for ever.[4]

Synge's old woman says, in the final words of the play, 'No man at all can be living for ever, and we must be satisfied' (III. 27).

These contrasts and parallels are such as to suggest that Synge was, in some ways, reacting against Yeats.

Riders to the Sea is certainly a more universal drama than Yeats' play; the imagery of it is so organized as to refer us, not only to the world of Irish history and folklore, but also to the world of archetypal symbolism. It has been said that the sea is the main protagonist in the drama. An exchange early in the play juxtaposes references to the sea and to God:

NORA: . . . the Almighty God won't leave her destitute . . . with no son living.
CATHLEEN: Is the sea bad by the white rocks, Nora?
NORA: Middling bad, God help us.   (III. 5–7)

The references to God in this play are, however, less precise than those to aspects of the landscape and the life of the characters. The points of the compass are used to emphasize the island-nature of the locale, but also for other reasons. Michael has been found in 'the far North' (III. 5); the wind is 'rising from the south and west' (III. 7). In the east, however, where the main-land lies, there may be hope for 'the tide's turning at the green head, and the hooker's tacking from the east' (III. 7), and it is from this direction that Maurya believes Michael's body will come, rather than from the north. This emphasis upon the dominance of the sea makes the sea itself into a power, a god. One recalls the sea god, Poseidon, for the death of Bartley is not unlike the death of Hippolitus; the latter had a more severe disagreement with his mother, of course, but he certainly left the house without her blessing, having rejected her incestuous love.

MAURYA: Isn't it a hard and cruel man, won't hear a word from an old woman, and she holding him from the sea?
CATHLEEN: It's the life of a young man to be going on the sea, and who would listen to an old woman with one thing and she saying it over?
BARTLEY: I must go now quickly. I'll ride on the red mare, and the grey pony'll run behind me. . . . The blessing of God on you.

MAURYA: He's gone now, God spare us, and we'll not see him again. He's gone now, and when the black night is in it I'll have no son living in the world.

CATHLEEN: Why wouldn't you give him your blessing and he looking back in the door? Isn't it sorrow enough is on every one in this house without your sending him out with an unlucky word behind him, and a hard word in his ear? (III. 11)

It was the 'hard word' of Phaedra that led to Theseus taking up his option on the three wishes given him by Poseidon and causing the horses of Hippolitus to be startled by a sea-beast and his horse to throw him to his death.

Synge has not done more than utilize the basic pattern of the myth; he has made no explicit allusions. Nevertheless the emphasis of the play upon such design, and upon mythic feeling is clear. Every detail contributes something. The pig with the black feet appears to be the family's only asset. The pig is in mythology sacred both to the moon-goddess (who rules the sea) and to the death-goddess, for it is an eater of corpses. Swine in Irish mythology are thought to belong to the Other World. Moreover, it is Manannan mac Lir who instituted the Faeth Fiadha at which the 'Pigs of Manannan' are to be 'killed and yet continue to exist for warriors'. Manannan mac Lir is a god of the sea.

The use of number is also significant in this play. Michael was missing for nine days. Maurya, like Niobe, wept 'nine days' for her lost son. Maurya herself, recalling the drowning of Patch, reports that she saw 'two women, and three women, and four women coming in' (III. 21). This adds up to nine again, as do the numbers mentioned by Bartley himself when he says optimistically 'you'll see me coming again in two days, or in three days, or maybe in four days if the wind is bad' (III. 11). Eight men have been drowned of Maurya's household, her husband's father, her husband, and her six sons; the ninth death will, it is implied, be Maurya's own. The banqueting hall at Tara had nine chambers; these, it has been suggested, represented the eight main points of the compass and the central point.

The number nine is one familiar to all students of mythology. It is a triple trinity and therefore a perfect number. An early draft of the play has Maurya stating 'in three nights it is Martin's night' (III. 244). Martinmas falls on 11 November so that the day of the play's action must be 9 November. November itself is, as its name indicates, the ninth month of the ancient Roman calendar. Later versions of the play, however, suggest that the action takes place some time before Samhain, which is November Eve or Hallowe'en, the time when ghosts may walk and demons plague the earth, for Maurya says, after the death of Bartley, 'I'll have no call now to be going down and getting Holy Water in the dark nights after Samhain. . . . It's a great rest I'll have now and great sleeping in the long nights after Samhain' (III. 25).

Although the first complete draft of the play includes no nines, and no ghosts, the element of myth and superstition is still very much present. Martinmas is emphasized as a time of death (it is the slaughtering season). Patch says, 'In three nights it is Martin's night and it is from this house a sheep must be killed' (III. 244). In this version of the play Patch is drowned when he and another man 'were going after the hooker and [he] and another man leaned out to hit at them black birds with his oar, and when he did it a wave came behind them and upset them and it took Patch and washed him back by the rocks and he was drowned there' (III. 248). These black birds can be identified from *The Aran Islands*, where an old man tells Synge a story:

Well, one Sunday a man came down and said there was a big ship coming into the sound. I ran down with two men and we went out in a curagh; we went round the point where they said the ship was, and there was no ship in it. As it was a Sunday we had nothing to do, and it was a fine calm day, so we rowed out a long way looking for the ship till I was further than I ever was before or after. When I wanted to turn back we saw a great flock of birds on the water and they all black, without a white bird through them. They had no fear of us at all, and the men with me wanted to go up to them, so we went further. When we were quite close they got up, so many that they blackened the sky, and they lit down again a hundred or maybe a hundred and twenty yards off. We went after them again, and one of the men wanted to kill one with his rowing stick. I was afraid they would upset the curagh, but they would go after the birds.

When we were quite close one man threw the pin and the other man hit at them with his rowing stick, and the two of them fell over in the curagh, and she turned on her side and only it was quite calm the lot of us were drowned.

I think those black gulls and the ship were the same sort, and after that I never went out as a pilot. It is often curaghs go out to ships and find there is no ship. (II. 181)

Although the black birds do not appear in the final version of the play, their use in the early version shows just how intent Synge was upon imbuing his play with mythic and supernatural feeling. In Irish legend supernatural beings often take the form of sea birds, and gulls are believed to be the souls of the drowned. If the 'black birds' do not appear in the final version, there is a reference to 'the black hags that do be flying on the sea' (III. 17), and Bartley is on his way to see the ship when he is killed. In the paragraph immediately preceding the one I have just quoted we read another of the old man's stories:

'There do be strange things on the sea,' he said. 'One night I was down there where you can see that green point, and I saw a ship coming in and I wondered what it would be doing coming so close to the rocks. It came straight on towards the place I was in, and then I got frightened and I ran up to the houses, and when the captain saw me running he changed his course and went away.' (II. 181)

The implication here, of course, is that the ship was attempting to lure the man to his death, or maybe to a strange voyage. Nora tells Cathleen that 'the tide's turning at the green head, and the hooker's tacking from the east' (III. 7). A little later she says, 'She's passing the green head, and letting fall her sails' (III. 11). Bartley's next speech is filled with dramatic irony:

I'll have half an hour to go down, and you'll see me coming again, in two days, or in three days, or maybe in four days if the wind is bad. (III. 11)

The death of Bartley is developed from several passages in *The Aran Islands*. The passage most usually regarded as important is that noted by Dr Saddlemyer:

When the horses were coming down to the slip an old woman saw her son, that was drowned a while ago, riding on one of them. She didn't say what she was after seeing, and this man caught the horse, he caught his own horse first, and then he caught this one, and after that he went out and was drowned. (II. 164)

Dr Saddlemyer also refers to another story by the old man in which a young woman's ghost returns to her cottage to feed her child:

She told them she was away with the fairies, and they could not keep her that night, though she was eating no food with the fairies, the way she might be able to come back to her child. Then she told them they would all be leaving that part of the country on the Oidhche Shamhna, and that there would be four or five hundred of them riding on horses, and herself would be on a grey horse, riding behind a young man. And she told them to go down to a bridge they would be crossing that night, and to wait at the head of it, and when she would be coming up she would slow the horse and they would be able to throw something on her and on the young man and they would fall over on the ground and be saved. (II. 159)

There is a third passage which also relates to this theme of the traveller being followed by a ghost horse. The old man says:

One night when he was coming home from the lighthouse he heard a man riding on the road behind him, and he stopped to wait for him, but nothing came. Then he heard as if there were a man trying to catch a horse on the rocks, and in a little time he went on. The noise behind him got bigger as he went along as if twenty horses and then as if a hundred or a thousand, were galloping after him. When he came to the stile where he had to leave the road and got over it, something hit against him and threw him down on the rock, and a gun he had in his hand fell into the field beyond him. (II. 180)

The notion of a large number of horses is associated with death by Maurya when she says:

If it was a hundred horses, or a thousand horses you had itself, what is the price of a thousand horses against a son where there is one son only? (III. 9)

It is worth noting that in the above stories the man escaped his fate once at a bridge and once at a stile. Both bridges and stiles have many associations with faerie and the protection from faerie. In *Riders to the Sea* Cathleen advises Maurya to go down to intercept Bartley at the 'spring well', and then 'the dark word will be broken' (III. 13). Maurya, however, is so astonished by the spectre of Michael that she cannot give Bartley her protective blessing.

In choosing to abandon the 'black birds' and Martinmas motifs and replace them with the 'ghost horse' and Samhain ones, Synge obviously intended to emphasize less the finality of death and slaughter than the world of spectre and spirit. Thus in the later drafts of the play Michael's body is discovered before cock-crow (when apparitions are all banished). Nora tells Cathleen that the young priest said:

There were two men . . . and they rowing round with poteen before the cocks crowed and the oar of one of them caught the body, and they passing the black cliffs of the North. (III.13–14)

In classical mythology there is a place of darkness through which spirits pass into Hades. Black cliffs occur as ominous places in many folk-tales and myths.

This, of course, connects up with the appearance of Michael's apparition later in the play, riding a grey pony. The colour grey is associated with death in Ireland. The Grey Washer by the Ford is, in Irish folk-tale, a female spectre who seems at first to be washing clothes in a river, but when approached by the man about to die she holds up the clothes and they have become the man's own phantom marked with the mortal wounds he is about to receive. Here the use of clothing and spectre echoes Synge's treatment of the appearance of Michael. It should also be pointed out that in *Revelations* VI. 8 'the Pale Horse' stands for Death, that Sleipnir, Odin's grey horse, typified the wild wind, and that as Poseidon, the sea-god, created the horse, so horse-farmers must be regarded as servants of Poseidon (or possibly of the moon-goddess, Demeter, to whom horses were also sacred).

That Synge was aware of the universal nature of the symbolism he was using, can hardly be doubted. In a review of H. d'Arbois de Jubainville's *The Irish Mythological Cycle and Celtic Mythology* printed in *The Speaker* of 2 April 1904, Synge reveals his long-time familiarity with this material, and refers to the 'Greek kinship of these Irish legends' (II. 365), and illustrates his comment by suggesting that Lug is a Celtic Hermes and Balor the Chimaera. He also mentions 'Manannan mac Lir, an Irish sea god' (II. 365). In a review of Lady Gregory's *Cuchulain of Muirthemne* in *The Speaker* of 7 June 1902, Synge again compares Celtic with Homeric story, and here he says: 'The Elizabethan vocabulary has a force and colour that make it the only form of English that is quite suitable for incidents of the epic kind, and in her intercourse with the peasants of the west Lady Gregory has learned to use this vocabulary in a new way, while she carries with her plaintive Gaelic constructions that make her language, in a true sense, a language of Ireland' (II. 368). This passage indicates pretty clearly what Synge was about when he filled *Riders to the Sea* with mythic intimations and reveals also that, even while he was concerned to present accurately the life and dignity of the Aran peasant, he was also interested in creating a more universal picture of man surrounded by natural elements and super-natural forces – or beliefs about those supernatural forces – which he is unable to control.

Seen from this viewpoint, *Riders to the Sea* takes on something of a new identity. The very title itself emphasizes the mythic or supernatural element for there are only two riders in the play, one the doomed Bartley and the other his spectral brother. We are all, Maurya tells us, doomed to death, for 'no man can be living for ever'. We are all, sooner or later, called to destruction. It is one of the messages of Greek tragedy, and the form of the play has much in common with Greek theatre. The climactic action takes place off-stage and is commented upon by Maurya, who returns, distraught with her forebodings, as the Greek chorus returns similarly distraught in so many plays. The old women keening just before the news of Bartley's death is told, function like a Greek chorus, as also do the two women who describe Bartley's death. In the Houghton typescript, which is certainly an earlier version than the established text, the stage directions give their speeches under the heading WOMEN rather than ONE OF THE WOMEN which is the heading in all published versions.

The dramatic irony in the play is also similar to that found in Greek tragedy. Nora reports the priest's words thus: 'she'll be getting her death' says he 'with crying and lamenting' (III. 5): it is, indeed, Maurya's lamenting Bartley's going down to the ship that prevents her from giving her blessing and thus causes his death. A simpler, but still classical, use of foreboding speech occurs when Maurya says to Bartley:

It's hard set we'll be surely the day you're drowned with the rest. What way will I live and the girls with me, and I an old woman looking for the grave? (III. 11)

After a further passage of foreboding, irony returns with a play upon the vernacular usage of the word 'destroyed'. Nora says:

And it's destroyed he'll be going till dark night, and he after eating nothing since the sun went up. (III. 11)

Cathleen reinforces the effect:

It's destroyed he'll be, surely. (III. 13)

The pathos and dignity of Maurya's speech on taking Michael's stick to assist her steps as she goes to the spring to give her blessing to Bartley is not unlike many of the laments in Aeschylus, Sophocles, and Euripides.

In the big world the old people do be leaving things after them for their sons and children, but in this place it is the young men do be leaving things behind them for them that do be old. (III. 13)

The emphasis in this speech upon the way in which the world of Maurya differs from the 'big world' appears to set the island community apart from all other communities. Moreover, while in Greek tragedy and story the suffering of the protagonists is the consequence of the sins they or their kin have committed, intentionally or otherwise, in *Riders to the Sea* there appears to be no reason for Maurya's tribulation. The deaths of her sons are not, as are the deaths of Niobe's children, or Medea's, the consequence of acts of blasphemy or evil. In this, *Riders to the Sea* is closer to the world of Sophocles than Euripides; there is an arbitrary quality about the fates of the characters that reminds one of the world of Oedipus. Even here, however, one can find some historical justification for the cruelty of the fates. In *Riders to the Sea*, however, there is no justification. This is not a place in which there is any kind of justice, or mercy. The priest may say that 'the Almighty God won't leave her [Maurya] destitute with no son living' (III. 5.), but Maurya tells us, 'It's little the like of him knows of the sea' (III. 21). The sea is, indeed, the 'Almighty God' of the play, an older and more formidable spiritual power than that represented by the priest who, it is emphasized, is 'young'. The priest never enters the action of the play. He is absent physically from the cottage of Maurya just as he is, spiritually, a stranger to her world. His reported words are all comforting, but they do not comfort.

Yet it may be suggested that Christianity plays a part in the play. Does not Maurya sprinkle 'Holy Water' over the clothes of the drowned Michael?

This may be so, but there is some doubt as to the nature of that 'Holy Water', for Maurya refers to 'going down and getting Holy Water in the dark nights after Samhain' (III. 25). It may be that she collects it from a Holy Well, even the Spring Well, mentioned in the play, but it is clear that the only time she does collect it is in the nights after Samhain, for now that Samhain is nearly come round again her supply is almost exhausted; it is the last of the Holy Water she sprinkles over Michael's clothes. Thus the Holy Water is much more the magical water of pre-Christian belief than the water blessed by the priest. Indeed, the priest is not in it at all.

The fusion of pre-Christian and Christian belief is characteristic, of course, of many peasant communities. Synge was not playing fast and loose with the facts. He was, however, portraying a world in which people, insecure and desperate for help against the forces of death and the tyranny of the natural world, seized upon any belief or superstition that might give them comfort and hope. That Maurya finds no comfort or hope for all her observances is the dark message of the play, which ends as a cry, not against God, but against the principle of Mortality. 'No man can be living for ever and we must be satisfied' (III. 27).

If this humble, even partly stoic, conclusion of Maurya's is set against the conclusion of Yeats' *Cathleen ni Houlihan*, together with all the other elements in the play that I have mentioned, it becomes clear in just what way *Riders to the Sea* is a counterblast to Yeats. Synge was certainly very much aware that his view of Ireland differed from that of Yeats. Some of his poems seem to be direct retorts to Yeats' early lyrics. On 12 September 1907 he wrote, in a letter to the Irish-American journalist, Frederick J. Gregg: 'I am half inclined to try a play on "Deirdre" – it would be amusing to compare it with Yeats' and Russell's . . .' (IV. xxvii). *Deirdre of the Sorrows* is, certainly, in many ways constructed so as to oppose the vision of Yeats with another. It is therefore not unreasonable to look again at *Riders to the Sea* in these terms.

Cathleen ni Houlihan is, of course, a personification of Ireland, an old woman (the Shan Van Vocht) who has the 'step of a queen'. Maurya, also an old woman, is not an allegorical but a typical figure; she too mourns the past dead though her step is not that of a queen, but weak with age. Cathleen ni Houlihan mourns the loss of her 'four fields' – the four provinces of Ireland. Maurya mourns the loss of her eight menfolk, but without the triumphant tone of Yeats' Old Woman. The ship that brings hope of Irish freedom to Yeats' characters, brings death to the characters of Synge. *Riders to the Sea* is, indeed, a comprehensive drama. It includes, at a more profound level than *Cathleen ni Houlihan*, an awareness of the Irish inheritance of story and belief. Its portrait of the island is that of a place shut off from the 'big world', as Ireland itself is shut off. It is a portrait of a place bewildered by two cultures, the ancient and the new, and by two visions of the nature of the spiritual world.

The island of *Riders to the Sea* is Ireland, but more than Ireland. Its predicaments are those of the Irish peasant, but also those of all men subject to the tyranny of forces they do not understand. Its beliefs are those of the Irish peasant, but they are also those of all people who combine superstition with Christian belief, or who are troubled by thoughts of spiritual realities beyond their ability to understand and control. *Riders to the Sea* is not naturalistic theatre; it is poetic theatre, and it is epic. The figure of man placed against the power of the gods who destroy him is a main theme of epic and of heroic tragedy. Maurya, like Oedipus, bows to the will of the gods, and, like Job, finds at last in humility and endurance a dignity and greatness of spirit, turning down the empty cup of Holy Water in a last symbolic gesture, and asking for mercy upon the souls of all mortal kind.

CHAPTER FIVE

The Shadow of the Glen

The Shadow of the Glen was begun in the summer of 1902 at a time when Synge was also working on *Riders to the Sea*. It was completed during 1903, first produced at the Molesworth Hall on 8 October of that year, and first printed in *Samhain* in December 1904. This version was, however, revised, and the final text did not appear until May 1905 when it was published alongside *Riders to the Sea*.

Although it was the first of Synge's plays to be staged, it has, as yet, received much less critical attention than its companion, and the reasons for this comparative neglect are easy to understand. In the first place, it might appear on the surface to be little more than a dramatized anecdote whose main interest is the vitality and richness of the dialect in which it is written. In the second place, it does not have the mythic universality of *Riders to the Sea*; and nor, in the third place, does it achieve the vitality of Synge's later comedies. It is, however, in reality, a subtle and complex construction in which Synge for the first time develops that ironic ambiguity of tone which makes the later and rightly celebrated *Playboy of the Western World* so fascinating.

The Shadow of the Glen was developed from a story told to Synge by Pat Dirane, the old shanachie of Inishmaan, in 1898. This story, in a somewhat polished version, was included in *The Aran Islands* (1907), but the original draft of it can now be found in Volume Three of the Oxford University Press edition of Synge's Collected Works (pp. 254–6). This version can easily be summarized. The shanachie tells how, on a rainy night, while

53

travelling from Galway to Dublin, he came across a house in which a solitary woman sat watching a man laid out on a bed as if he were dead. The woman gave the shanachie shelter and asked him to watch by the corpse while she went out to tell her friends of the death. When the woman had gone the 'corpse' sat up and told the shanachie, 'I've got a bad wife so I let on to be dead the way I'd catch her at her goings on.' The woman returned to the cottage with a young man whom she sent into the bedroom to rest. In a little while she joined the young man in the bedroom. The husband waited for a few minutes and then got out of bed and took up a stick and gave the shanachie another, and both men went into the bedroom, and when they saw the wife and her companion together, the husband 'hit the young man with the stick so that his blood lept up and hit the gallery'.

In modifying this story for the stage Synge brought it closer to the classical folk-tale of the Widow of Ephesus, and gave those who felt the dubious morality of his characters to be un-Irish an excuse to accuse him of placing an essentially alien story in an Irish context and thus falsifying the picture of rural Ireland. On 11 February 1905 Synge responded to this accusation with a letter to *The United Irishman*:

Sir, I beg to enclose the story of an unfaithful wife which was told me by an old man on the middle island of Aran in 1898, and which I have since used in a modified form in *The Shadow of the Glen*. It differs essentially from any version of the story of the Widow of Ephesus with which I am acquainted. As you will see, it was told to me in the first person, as not infrequently happens in folktales of this class. Yours &tc., J. M. Synge.   (III. 254)

This letter is somewhat disingenuous. It does not actually deny that the dramatized version of the story resembles that of the Widow of Ephesus, as, clearly, in some respects it does; it only suggests that the source material was native rather than alien. It also shows that Synge was familiar with the Widow of Ephesus story, and, this being the case, he could hardly have failed to recognize the similarities between the two tales. In 1905, however, it was not a time to suggest that folk-tales tend to be universal; Irish nationalism was rampant and insistent upon the unique nature of Irish culture. Nor would it have been wise of Synge to admit that in revising the original story he had deliberately brought it closer in both mood and plot to the classical folk-tale. Nevertheless, all we know of Synge's interest in comparative mythology and the study of folklore points to his being aware that the shanachie's story was but one version of a widespread tale, and suggests that his modifications of his original may, at least in part, have been caused by a wish to emphasize the universality of his theme.

This may all seem a matter of relatively little importance until we consider the relationship of this play to the other work Synge was writing during that same summer of 1902. During that year he drafted three plays, *Riders to the Sea*, *The Shadow of the Glen*, and *The Tinker's Wedding*. Each of these plays is so constructed as to echo story-patterns which have long existed in Western culture: the death of Bartley in *Riders to the Sea* echoes the story of Hippolitus; the plot of *The Shadow of the Glen* utilizes the Widow of Ephesus pattern; and the story of *The Tinker's Wedding* has a generic similarity to the type of folk material utilized by Boccaccio and Chaucer. Each play, also, is based upon material given Synge by the Irish peasantry.

Indeed, it would hardly be wrenching the facts to describe these three plays as forming a trilogy. The earliest drafts of *The Tinker's Wedding* show that it also began as a one-act play, and in the first complete version of 1903 the old woman's version of the freedom of the tinker's life strongly resembles the final speech of the tramp in *The Shadow of the Glen*. The old woman says:

What is it the Almighty God would care of the like of us? You'ld never see the Almighty doing a thing to the larks or to the swallows or to the swift birds do be crying out when the sun is set, or to the hares do be racing above in the fine spring, and what way would he be following us in the dark nights, when it's quiet and easy we are, and we never asking him a thing at all?

(IV. 279)

The tramp says:

Come along with me now, lady of the house, and it's not my blather you'll be hearing only, but you'll be hearing the herons crying out over the black lakes, and you'll be hearing the grouse, and the owls with them, and the larks and the big thrushes when the days are warm, and it's not from the like of them you'll be hearing a talk of getting old like Peggy Cavanagh, and

55

losing the hair off you, and the light of your eyes, but it's fine songs you'll
be hearing when the sun goes up, and there'll be no old fellow wheezing the
like of a sick sheep close to your ear.   (III. 54)

Moreover, the central themes of all three plays can be related to
each other. In all three there is the conflict between folk belief
and conventional Christian attitudes. In all three we are shown
a woman trapped by circumstances, and in each one we are
presented with a different aspect of her predicament. In *Riders to
the Sea* the old woman, the mother figure, broods over the
solitude to which she has come at the death of her menfolk. In
The Shadow of the Glen the still young wife is trapped by the
solitude of the glens and by her loveless marriage, and is stirred
by a desire for freedom. In *The Tinker's Wedding* Sarah Casey,
the young tinker woman, desires to become a bride and to join
the ranks of accepted wives, in spite of the advice of old Mary
Byrne who stands for the traditionally anarchic freedom of her
pagan breed. In all three cases conventional ideas of the 'big
world' are challenged, and the play's central figure feels herself
the victim of forces she cannot control. The priest in *Riders to
the Sea* is regarded as knowing little of the ways of the sea-torn
world. The convention of marriage in *The Shadow of the Glen* is
opposed to the lyricism of the human heart and the needs of the
human spirit. And in *The Tinker's Wedding* the priest proves to
be shallow and imperceptive.

Not only do these three plays have thematic links, they also
form a kind of progression. As we proceed from *Riders to the Sea*,
through *The Shadow of the Glen* to *The Tinker's Wedding*, the age
of the central female character diminishes and the psychological
complexity of the drama increases. In *Riders to the Sea* the
characters are simple, each dominated by a single emotional
attitude. In *The Shadow of the Glen* Nora and the Tramp are more
varied in their emotional reactions to events. In *The Tinker's
Wedding* the two female characters are more complex still and
the subsidiary characters less predictable. The fourth of these
plays of the Irish countryside, the plays which I like to label collec-
tively as 'the shanachie plays', is *The Playboy of the Western World*,
in which the majority of the characters are fully individuated.

There is also in these three plays a mounting tide of rebellion.

The four shanachie plays all have in common their use of a central female character who is the voice of the play's energy. The conflict is centred in her words and her confusions. In *Riders to the Sea* the woman, Maurya, becomes resigned to her fate, and the epic mood of the play prevents niceties of psychological shading. *The Shadow of the Glen*, however, gives us, in Nora Burke, a more complex character hovering upon the edge of outright rebellion, while Sarah Casey in *The Tinker's Wedding* is the passionate protagonist of the play's action and outspoken in her rejection of her condition. The Christian ethos, dismissed as irrelevant in *Riders to the Sea*, is faced and opposed in *The Shadow of the Glen*, and ridiculed outrageously in *The Tinker's Wedding*. Religious beliefs, moral standards, and conventional social attitudes are tackled with increasing vigour and insistence as the plays proceed. In addition, as these first three shanachie plays progress they become more humorous: the first is tragic, the second tragi-comic, and the third farcical.

If we look at the shanachie plays in these various ways it becomes apparent that *The Shadow of the Glen* is a transitional play involving crucial artistic decisions. It is in this play that the main themes of Synge's drama are first effectively, though perhaps summarily, displayed, and the main varieties of his characterization suggested. As has already been pointed out, *The Shadow of the Glen* is dominated by the personality of a woman, Nora Burke. The three men are no more than her foils, and two of them are stock figures. Dan Burke, the old husband, is a possessive man who cannot bear his young wife even to speak to other men, and who is derisive of her expressions of emotion. Michael Dara is a superstitious and timid youth interested in Nora only for her land and money. Only when he is assured that she can bring him material wealth does he put his arm round her and say, 'It's a fine life you'll have now with a young man, a fine life surely' (III. 53). These two represent the complacent male materialism against which Synge set restless female idealism in several of his plays. It is not, indeed, Irish womanhood that is being attacked here, but Irish manhood. John Butler Yeats saw the point, and said in a letter to *The United Irishman* that the play was:

... a very effective attack on loveless marriages – the most miserable institution so dear to our thrifty elders among the peasants and among their
betters, by whom anything like impulse or passion is discredited, human
nature coerced at every point and sincerity banished from the land. . . .[5]

The third male character, the tramp, is more complex than the
others, partly because it is he who attempts to justify impulse
and passion. He is also more observant; he registers the 'queer
look' (III. 33) of the dead man, and notices immediately that
the corpse has not been properly laid out. He gently hints at his
own sexual vitality by telling Nora that many a woman would
be 'afeard of the like of me in the dark night' (III. 37). He himself is uneasy about the corpse and the possibility of ghosts, and
begs a needle which he can put under his lapel as a protection
against the shade of Patch Darcy, and when left alone with the
corpse he says the De Profundis, an established means of warding
off evil spirits (III. 41). He is quick to adapt himself to new
situations: when Dan reveals his subterfuge he soon accepts the
role he is to play. Sharp-tongued, he derides Michael's inepti-
tude with the mountain ewes, and he is outspokenly opposed to
Dan's brutal attitude towards Nora. At the end of the play he
gives Nora hope and dignity with his description of her future
life on the roads, and his last words are scornful of the old
husband, for, he says 'there'll be no old fellow wheezing the like
of a sick sheep close to your ear' (III. 57). The tramp, indeed,
acts as the focal sensibility of the play without ever straying
from his role as a character within it. Like Michael, he is
superstitious, but, unlike Michael, he does not retreat before the
unusual. It is he who forces Nora into full understanding of her
situation by saying of Michael, 'Maybe himself would take her'
(III. 55), piling this Pelion upon the Ossa of Michael's own
suggestion of the 'Union below in Rathdrum' (III. 55) as a
home for his erstwhile prospective wife.

The tramp is, finally, a means for Nora to find herself. He
stimulates her to open admission of her feelings, and in his
lyrical description of the freedom of the wandering life he gives
language to the impulse towards freedom which she herself has
shown in her dealings with men and in her open resentment of
the narrow confines of her life. (This is not to say that his praise

of the vagrant life is merely a dramatic device, it is an accurate presentation of the feelings of many vagrants of his kind; his romanticism is copied from life and not invented for thematic purposes.)

Nora herself is a complex character. Alone with a corpse, she shows courage and even humour, though she also reveals her belief in the efficacy of curses. She is candid about her unhappiness and unafraid of admitting her sexual frustration to a stranger, saying of her husband, 'he was always cold, every day since I knew him – and every night . . .' (III. 35). She reveals a degree of self-conceit and sexual aggressiveness in her boast, 'I never knew what way I'd be afeared of beggar or bishop or any man of you at all' (III. 37), and the contrast of this remark with her earlier rhetorical question, 'how would I go out into the glen and tell the neighbours and I a lone woman with no house near me?' (III. 37), makes us wonder if there may not be another reason for her remaining in the house. She betrays her interest in men by her sad reference to Patch Darcy and her loneliness after his death. Her sexual hunger and frustration is clearly shown by her next two sentences: first she says, 'then I got happy again – if it's ever happy we are, stranger – for I got used to being lonesome', and then adds, after a pause, 'Was there anyone on the last bit of the road, stranger, and you coming from Aughrim?' (III. 39). Her insistence on going out herself to find the young man, and her wish to have the tramp rest in the other room while she and Michael talk further reveal her needs. We are not told explicitly that she is adulterous or promiscuous. It is, however, beautifully implied. The tramp accuses Michael of being a 'poor herd'. Michael admits his problems with his 'little handful of ewes':

It's no lie he's telling, I was destroyed surely. . . . They were that wilful they were running off into one man's bit of oats, and another man's bit of hay, and tumbling into the red bogs till it's more like a pack of old goats than sheep they were. . . . Mountain ewes is a queer breed, Nora Burke, and I'm not used to them at all. (III. 47)

Goats are proverbially lecherous, and the juxtaposition of the phrase 'mountain ewes' with the name of Nora is suggestive. Nora's response is equally significant:

There's no one can drive a mountain ewe but the men do be reared in the Glen Malure, I've heard them say, and above by Rathvanna, and the Glen Imaal, men the like of Patch Darcy. . . . (III. 47)

Patch Darcy, she and the tramp agree, was a 'great man', and it is impossible not to regard him as the 'herd' who had shown himself most capable of controlling that wild 'mountain ewe', Nora, and keeping her from other men's 'oats' and 'hay'. This interpretation is reinforced by the following dialogue between Nora and Michael:

MICHAEL *looking at her with a queer look*: I heard tell this day, Nora Burke, that it was on the path below Patch Darcy would be passing up and passing down, and I heard them say he'd never pass it night or morning without speaking with yourself.

NORA *in a low voice*: It was no lie you heard, Michael Dara.

MICHAEL *as before*: I'm thinking it's a power of men you're after knowing if it's in a lonesome place you live itself. (III. 47–8)

Here the dialect usage of 'if' meaning 'though' plays into Synge's hands, for it results in an apparently paradoxical statement, and yet one which points to the fact that it is the lonely and desolate who find it necessary to seek out emotional relationships and, perhaps, accept any that come their way. Nevertheless, the hungers born of such emotional starvation are hard to satisfy. Nora herself makes the point:

NORA *slowly, giving him his tea*: It's in a lonesome place you do have to be talking with someone, and looking for someone, in the evening of the day, and if it's a power of men I'm after knowing they were fine men, for I was a hard child to please, and a hard girl to please (*she looks at him a little sternly*) and it's a hard woman I am to please this day, Michael Dara, and it's no lie, I'm telling you. (III. 49)

Michael here asks the obvious question and reveals for us the nature of the trap which is marriage in the glens:

MICHAEL *looking over to see that the Tramp is asleep and then, pointing to the dead man*: Was it a hard woman to please you were when you took himself for your man?

NORA: What way would I live and I an old woman if I didn't marry a man with a bit of a farm, and cows on it, and sheep on the back hills? (III. 49)

This, though spoken as a rhetorical question, is one of the real questions asked and answered in the play. Nora herself surveys the situation as she listlessly counts the money in the house. On the one hand she envies those married women who have children to qualify their loneliness. On the other hand she thinks of 'Peggy Cavanagh' walking the roads in poverty, and is fearful of the consequences of that freedom for which she yearns. Michael's interest in her as prospective wife increases as the pile of money grows, and when the sum of 'five pounds and ten notes' (III. 51) is reached he suggests marriage.

Nora's reaction is interesting. Though earlier she has expressed envy of Mary Brien who has 'two children and another coming on her in three months or four', she does not think of marriage to a young man as being likely to produce children, but sees it as an abandonment of whatever youth and exuberance she has left:

Why would I marry you, Mike Dara? You'll be getting old, and I'll be getting old, and in a little while, I'm telling you, you'll be sitting up in your bed – the way himself was sitting – with a shake in your face, and your teeth falling, and the white hair sticking out round you like an old bush where sheep do be leaving a gap. (III. 51)

Her sexual frustration is not the only source of her confusion and despair. She also feels herself trapped by time itself.

It is here that one of Synge's central motifs appears clearly for the first time in his mature drama. In all the completed plays from this time onward he presented a central character animated by a desire for the zestful enjoyment of life's pleasures and anxious at the passing of time and the inevitable approach of death. These characters are afflicted by an inability to avoid taking the long view even while emphasizing the possible delights of the present. The beggars in *The Well of the Saints* look towards an ideal future as desperately and as yearningly as Pegeen Mike in *The Playboy of the Western World*, and yet in all their talk of the future they implicitly deny the possibility of present laughter and offer an amulet to the face of death. In *The Shadow of the Glen* this predicament is presented with harsh clarity and with inescapable logic. The only pleasure possible in the present is, Nora realizes, a dream of the future, and that is simply a fantasy to ward off dread of what the future must finally bring.

61

Synge was mortality-conscious and time-haunted, and his characters present that double standard with which we deal with our unique human awareness of temporality. Nora may be the most obvious vehicle for this theme in the whole of Synge's drama, largely because she has for so long denied herself dreams and toughened herself by a steady contemplation of the cramping facts. Unlike *Deirdre of the Sorrows* she cannot accept a 'crowded hour of glorious life' in confidence that its value must exceed whatever price is to be paid for it. Unlike Maurya, of *Riders to the Sea*, she cannot resign herself to her fate. Unlike the Douls in *The Well of the Saints* she cannot lose herself in deliberate fantasy. Nor can she, like Sarah Casey of *The Tinker's Wedding*, rebel completely against the conventions, for her upbringing has not been that of a tinker girl. She has not the ruthless idealism of Pegeen Mike in search of her hero, for unlike Pegeen Mike she is sure that all her opportunities have been lost. She is, more than any other of Synge's heroines, a trapped and bitter figure, and the ironic note upon which the play ends is itself a tribute to that turbulence of spirit which gives her heroic stature even while it may also underline her moral frailty. The final words of the play, indeed, are an attack upon the poorness of spirit of the society in which she has spent her days, and an indication that there should be more to living than 'quiet' and 'good health'. Michael refers here once again to the 'mountain ewes' as sources of disturbance and brings Nora to our minds:

MICHAEL *coming back to the table*: And it's very dry I am surely, with the fear of death you put on me, and I after driving mountain ewes since the turn of the day.

DAN *throwing away his stick*: I was thinking to strike you, Michael Dara, but you're a quiet man, God help you, and I don't mind you at all.

He pours out two glasses of whiskey, and gives one to Michael.

DAN: Your good health, Michael Dara.

MICHAEL: God reward you, Daniel Burke, and may you have a long life and a quiet life, and good health with it.

They drink. (III. 59)

The Shadow of the Glen, though not utilizing the epic mood of *Riders to the Sea*, nevertheless presents a bitter predicament which would not have been inappropriate in Greek tragedy. One thinks of Medea, forced into infidelity by the fates and thereafter made criminal by circumstances and the abandonment of her tortured and proud spirit. The Widow of Ephesus, that stock figure of comedy, may also be recalled, but Synge, in a so-called comedy whose bitterness outraged its first audience, shows us that the Widow of Ephesus may also be a pathetic, even tragic, figure, and that the inevitability of fate which broods over Greek tragedy may also brood over the marital prisons of County Wicklow.

In *The Shadow of the Glen* Synge, far from mocking Irish problems, gave them dignity. The lyricism and bitterness of this play do indeed establish it as one of the most original works of the Irish Renaissance, the precursor of much black comedy, and the true forerunner of *Juno and the Paycock* and *Waiting for Godot*.

CHAPTER SIX

The Tinker's Wedding

Synge began work on *The Tinker's Wedding* in the summer of 1902, the period during which he was also writing *Riders to the Sea* and *The Shadow of the Glen*. He appears to have based his plot upon a story told him by a herd in Wicklow. This story he included in his essay *At a Wicklow Fair*. The herd, referring to a tinker with whom Synge had been chatting, says:

That man is a great villain. . . . One time he and his woman went up to a priest in the hills and asked him would he wed them for half a sovereign, I think it was. The priest said it was a poor price, but he'd wed them surely if they'd make him a tin can along with it. 'I will, faith,' said the tinker, 'and I'll come back when it's done.' They went off then, and in three weeks they came back, and they asked the priest a second time would he wed them. 'Have you the tin can?' said the priest. 'We have not' said the tinker; 'we had it made at the fall of night, but the ass gave it a kick this morning, the way it isn't fit for you at all.' 'Go on now,' says the priest. 'It's a pair of rogues and schemers you are, and I won't wed you at all.' They went off then, and they were never married to this day.　　　　　　　　　　　　(II. 228–9)

There is something a little curious about the timing of the publication of this essay. Synge wrote several essays about his travels through Ireland and his impressions of the people, and some of these were published in 1903 and 1904. In December 1904 Synge was given the opportunity to write pieces for the *Manchester Guardian*. His first contribution was an extract from his Aran book; this appeared on 24 January 1905. The *Manchester Guardian* then commissioned him to write a series of articles on the poorest areas of Galway and Mayo. These appeared in June–July 1905. He published two reviews in the paper during 1906, but the essay *At a Wicklow Fair* did not appear until 9 May

1907. It was during 1906 that the two-act version of *The Tinker's Wedding* was completed, and during 1907 that Synge began to think of publishing it as a book and drafted his preface to it. Thus it seems that Synge chose to publish an essay incorporating the apparent source material of his play at just about the same time that he completed the drama itself; it also seems that, if he had wished, he could easily have published it earlier. The essay's date of composition is given by Synge's nephew, Edward M. Stephens, as 1902–5. He may have been wrong.

This all might appear unimportant were it not that Synge had been disturbed in 1903 by the reaction to the production of *The Shadow of the Glen*, and especially by the accusation that the play was not based upon Irish, but upon foreign, material. It was in 1903 that Synge completed the first one-act draft of *The Tinker's Wedding* and considered the possibility of publishing it together with *Riders to the Sea* and *The Shadow of the Glen*. In January 1905 this plan was abandoned as Elkin Mathews felt that the two earlier plays made up a book of the right size for his series. It is worth noting, in passing, that Synge himself once saw these three plays as forming a possible unity. He may, there-fore, have been particularly inclined to ensure that the accusa-tion directed at *The Shadow of the Glen* should not be directed at *The Tinker's Wedding*, the third of his shanachie plays.

He and his friends were certainly very much aware of the likelihood of a bad reception for the play. On 9 September 1905 Yeats wrote that 'we may find it too dangerous for the theatre at present'. Synge, away from his papers, was afraid to ask his 'pious relations' to seek it out to send to Yeats 'for fear they would set fire to the whole' (IV. xiii). Yeats discussed the play with Synge and Willie Fay later in 1905 and told Lady Gregory that they were agreed that its production or even publication 'would be dangerous at present'. In 1906, writing to Max Meyerfeld, Synge described it as 'a little play written before the "Well of the Saints" but never played here because it is thought too immoral and anticlerical' (IV. xiv). Writing about it to Frank Sidgewick in August 1907, he said: 'We have never acted it here as it would have made a greater disturbance, if possible, than the "Playboy"' (IV. xv). On 28 November 1907 he wrote to

James Paterson: 'I am sending you a little play which I wrote some years ago but did not publish till the other day – The Tinker's Wedding – as you will understand we think it too dangerous to put it on in the Abbey – it is founded on a real incident that happened in Wicklow a few years ago' (IV. xvi). Not all Synge's letters have yet been published, and many have certainly been lost. On the present evidence, however, it looks as if it was only in 1907 that Synge first indicated that the play was based upon a true incident of Irish life.

This emphasis of Synge's upon the factual basis of his drama – he made the same claims about *The Shadow of the Glen* and *The Playboy of the Western World* – has led some writers to regard his work as an attempt at the naturalistic documentation of Irish life. Synge himself, however, wished the universal implications of his drama to be recognized. In *National Drama: A Farce*, which he wrote, in all probability, shortly after *The Shadow of the Glen* had been attacked, but which he never completed, he put his own views in the mouth of a character called Jameson. After a discussion in which various speakers demand that Irish drama should exhibit 'the virtue of its country', should 'have no sex' and that its authors should 'draw out their materials from the pearly depths of the Celtic imagination . . . leaving the naked truth a little to one side', Jameson makes two long speeches separated only by an interjection from Fogarty. The essence of his argument can be indicated easily by selective quotation:

In short you think that the Irish drama should hold up the mirror to the Irish Nation and it going to Mass on a fine springdayish Sunday morning? . . . I have not much to say. An Irish drama that is written in Ireland about Irish people, and not on a foreign model will and must be national in so far as it exists at all. Our hope of it is that as Ireland is a beautiful and lovely country that the drama that Ireland is now producing may catch a little of this beauty and loveliness, as the Irish music has caught it [without] knowing or thinking, and will escape the foolishness that all wilful national[ism] is so full of. . . . Art is sad or gay, religious or heretical, by reason of accident and cause we cannot account for and the small Tuscany produced at one time Dante and Boccaccio, who are surely both national and yet we feel that Dante might have been born in Paris or Rabelais in Venice. The national element in art is merely the colour, the intensity of the wildness or restraint of the humour. . . . I do not say that all artistic production is national – Gaelic adaptations (imitations) of fourth-rate English poetry are not national because they are not anything. . . . If you do not like a work that is passing itself off as national art you had better show that it is not art. If it is good art it is in vain for you to try and show that it is not national. . . . If we get drunk a little more in public than the other nations of Europe would you have us reeling on the stage in order that we may be national? no? Then if we have a few little fragments of local virtue must [they] be paraded in our button holes like a Gaelic button? The essentials of all art are the eternal human elements (coat sleeve) of humanity which are the same everywhere and it is only in the attributes that make an art more or less charged with beauty, more or less daring and exquisite in form, more or [less] dull or shiny on its surface, that the influence of place is to be found. . . . (III. 224–6)

This separation of 'attributes' from 'essentials' suggests that Synge, at the time when he was working on *The Tinker's Wedding*, and also, obviously, casting a backward look at *The Shadow of the Glen*, was concerned quite as much with the presentation of universal themes as with the accurate re-creation of local particulars. His attitude towards those who wrote with an eye more to the local than to the universal is indicated by his comment on Geoffrey Keating which he wrote in a review of Keating's *Foras Feasa Ar Eirinn: The History of Ireland*, published in *The Speaker* of 6 September 1902. 'Apart from his natural talent,' wrote Synge, 'he owes a good deal to his foreign studies . . . which gave him a knowledge of the outside prosperity of the world with which to compare the things he saw in Ireland' (II. 361). Later in the same review he said:

A comparison of the general expression of Keating's work with that of the annalists of his time recalls, in a curiously remote way, the difference that can be felt between the work of Irish writers of the present day who have spent part of their life in London or Paris, and the work of men who have not left Ireland. (II. 361)

Synge, we may remember, had lived in Paris. Another attack upon purely naturalistic and journalistic drama was made in a notebook of 1895–8:

Dramatic art is first of all a childish art – a reproduction of external experience – without form or philosophy; then after a lyrical interval we have it as mature drama dealing with the deeper truth of general life in a perfect form and with mature philosophy. (II. 350)

It may be presumed that anyone capable of making this statement would be incapable of, at least wittingly, presenting a drama of merely 'external experience'. External experience provided Synge with the attributes rather than the essentials of his work. The particular attributes of *The Tinker's Wedding* may have been derived from a tale heard in County Wicklow, or from general observation of the tinkers and vagrants described in several places in Synge's prose. The mood of the play, however, surely derives in part from a more general observation of Irish people, one which Synge made in a review of Seumas MacManus's *Donegal Fairy Stories* in *The Speaker* of 21 June 1902. After quoting a passage of MacManus's colloquial and racy prose, he wrote:

Such a style has a certain liveliness, yet when it is chosen by Irish writers, a great deal of what is most precious in the national life must be omitted from their work, or imperfectly expressed. On the other hand the rollicking note is present in the Irish character – present to an extent some writers of the day do not seem to be aware of – and it demands, if we choose to deal with it, a free rollicking style.   (II. 376)

It is tempting to believe that Synge was here not only thinking of the rollicking play which was in his own mind that summer, but also of the nationalist but non-rollicking work of Yeats and AE. The word 'free', however, deserves particular attention, for in *The Tinker's Wedding* Synge not only challenged the puritanical and 'wilful' nationalism of his time with a play he carefully showed to be based upon actual events, but also created a speech and dramatic movement whose apparent freedom from conventional formulae enables it the more powerfully and easily to embody profound and original intuitions of 'the deeper truth of general life'.

The form of *The Tinker's Wedding* was not achieved without a struggle. The first version occupies sixteen pages of a notebook in which there are also drafts of *Riders to the Sea* and *The Shadow of the Glen*. The first complete typescript draft is one of thirteen pages; this, like the notebook version, is a one-act play. The second typescript version is of two acts in forty pages, the third is of forty-four pages, and the fourth, fifth and sixth are all of thirty pages. Synge began with a relatively straightforward story: the tinkers sell the can that the priest asks for and tell him they have left it ready for him at Mrs Brady's house. He responds by telling them that he knows Mrs Brady is away in Kilgrade and that they are lying, and refuses to marry them. Even this simple version, however, reveals Synge's concern to derive general truth from particular situations, and to utilize symbolism. The young tinker woman, here called Nora, and not Sarah, Casey, on being woken up at the very beginning of the play, says that she had been 'dreaming a fine dream of the priest' and tells the dream:

Himself was out on a big field and he with two wild geese yoked to a plough, but the devil a bit would they plough for him and he blessing them and cursing them again till they flew up into a river on the far [end] of Glen Macanass. (IV. 273)

This passage, slightly rewritten, appears also in the first typescript of the one-act version, but not in the final text. It may have been dropped because it suggests a too simple interpretation of the play which is, in fact, about more than the recalcitrance of the wild Irish. Moreover, the phrase 'wild geese' reminds one of the soldiers of Patrick Sarsfield who were given that nickname, and therefore has irrelevant secondary associations. The dream, however, does indicate one of the themes which Synge was concerned to develop.

At the end of the first notebook draft there is another exchange which also does not appear in the final text, and, again, it is built around a single vivid image. After the priest has threatened to tell the police 'who it was stole the grey ass was belonging to Paddy O'Hea' and cause them to be thrown into gaol, the tinkers are angered and Mary Byrne says:

. . . Would you think it was a fine thing if you had that money away from us and what was [it] you'ld give us instead? You and your marriage! Isn't generations and generations we are walking round under the Heavens and what is it we ever wanted with [your like]? Let you not be talking. We have the hot suns and the cold night and our bits to eat and sups to drink and a power of children and what more is it we want. Is it rings we want when the frost does catch on our fingers. Let you listen to this. When a man parts with copper to put rings in a pig's nose and you'ld like us to pay you with the time you'ld put an old ring on ourselves. You would surely. Herself is a young woman and the young never know the things they want. I've had one husband and another husband and power of children God help them and it's little they or myself even with your old rings to help us on in the world.

Good day now your reverence and let you be putting rings on your own pigs and not minding ourselves it's ten generations I was saying we've been walking round on the roads and never a marriage in the family. (IV. 276–7)

In this rough draft the attack upon the outward forms of marriage and the resentment of any attempt to fetter human freedom are as simply anarchic as any presented by the uncompromisingly radical young people of our own day. The implication that the clergy regard their parishioners as beasts to be mistreated in the service of complete obedience to convention makes this early version of the play much more anti-clerical than the later ones.

Both these suppressed passages emphasize the spiritual and emotional freedom which is threatened by conventional morality. Synge was not only concerned to present this notion, however, and in the first typescript version (IV. 281–2) he introduced another theme by means of the tinker children:

1ST CHILD: We'll make a drum from this bit of a can the way we'll be like the green man we seen in the fair.
2ND CHILD: How would we be like the green man, and not a green rag on us at all?
1ST CHILD: We'll put a bit of rushes round our heads, and then we'll be like the green man surely, and it's a power of money we'll get for sweets beating that thing through the fair.
NORA *to* MICHAEL: Are you ready now I hear himself at the door?

Priest, fat man, comes down from the chapel.

The 'green man' is, of course, a figure much commented on in folklore studies, and it is generally agreed that he represents some aspect of pre-Christian beliefs and is probably a fertility figure. The green knight of *Gawayne and the Greene Knight*, and Robin Hood are two such, but there are many more. Thus the tinker children reveal to us that the ancient pre-Christian customs are part of their inheritance, and that they co-exist with Christianity. Unfortunately, however, in this version of the play the children only speak twice. The action opens with a child asking for money to buy sweets and being refused. The children do not speak again until they have the conversation given above. They therefore intrude arbitrarily upon the play and the effect is clumsy.

Synge was, however, very much attracted to the idea of using children to show the co-existence of ancient and modern attitudes in the play, and in the first draft of the two-act version of the play they turn up again. Michael asks them:

Did you set your eye, on a hen or a chicken, or a thing at all a man could eat?

Micky, one of the children, replies:

We seen two fine hens of Tim O'Flaherty's out rousting in the ash tree above the well, and they bending down the branch with the fat on them as if it was myself was climbing.

MICHAEL *to Nora who stands up*: If herself was come now with the porter we'ld have a right to pass round there for the hen this night, Nora Casey, for it'ld be a fine night to be out walking round with the Beauty of Ballinacree, and it's a long while since it was a good hen we had to eat.   (IV. 286)

This does not only indicate the tinkers' thieving propensities, however. It also shows that their amoral opportunism and their romanticism go hand in hand. The sensibility that enjoys a stolen roast hen also enjoys the thought of high romance. In this the tinkers may remind us of Synge's notebook comment that 'in all the poets the greatest . . . are supremely engrossed with life and yet with the wildness of their fancy . . .' (II. 347).

The wildness of the tinker's fancy is displayed in another passage of this draft.

Two little girls dressed for confirmation in white dresses pass down the road towards the chapel.

1ST GIRL *in a whisper*: The tinkers are in it.

2ND GIRL: They'll be gone please God, before the bishop will come up. What would he think at all, if he seen the like of them heathens sitting there doing their hairs by the door of the Church?

1ST GIRL: And it's that lot is the worst lot of the whole of them, Mary Kate, for I've heard tell it was the old one below in the ditch stripped off the better part of her clothes a while ago in Ballinacree, and beat two peelers, and they big men, fifty yards through the fair.

They go into the chapel railing

MARY: That's the first of the like of them I've seen this year Nora Casey, and it's as sure a sign of summer they are, God bless them, as the white tree over your head.

NORA *looking after them*: Wouldn't it be a grand thing to see Nanny, God help her, dressed up the like of one of them, and she walking up in the face of the Lord Bishop on a summer's day?

71

MARY: And wouldn't it be a fine thing to see yourself, Nora Casey, and you driving to the races in a gold coach, the like of the grand Lady Lieutenant. It's a finer woman you are surely. (IV. 287)

The little girls are both fascinated and appalled by the tinkers' way of life. They see them as 'heathen' and, because of their vulgar manners and appearance, likely to upset the representative of the God of white dresses and good manners. On the other hand, they are awed by the martial prowess of the old tinker woman. She herself regards the girls as signs of the season, almost as pre-Christian heralds of the summer, and does not consider the religious reasons for their dress. When Nora reveals her love of splendour by wishing that the little girl, Nanny, could be confirmed in a white dress, however, the old woman counters with a vision in which echoes of epic splendour are fused with references to contemporary eminence. The whole passage shows not only the difference between the views of the 'villagers' and those of the tinkers, but also a difference between the viewpoint of the two tinker generations. The elder sees glory in pagan, heroic and secular terms; the younger is attracted by the beauty and mystery of contemporary customs. Both, however, delight in dreams of romantic splendour, and those epic dreams may partly account for the outrageous, yet magnificently self-possessed, behaviour of the tribe.

Later in the same draft of the play the attitudes of the tinker children and the little girls are again compared. The 'green man' passage which first appeared in an earlier draft is repeated with only minor stylistic amendment and is followed by a conversation between the little girls.

1ST GIRL: Did you hear what the pig did last night, the pig Biddy's father was taking to the fair?
2ND GIRL: I did not.
1ST GIRL: It's after tearing the front out of her frock, and there she is now getting her death fretting, and she with nothing to put on her at all.
2ND GIRL: They bought that pig from the old minister and I'm thinking the devil was in it. Didn't you ever hear of the devils going down into the swine?
2ND GIRL: An old daddy goat is the devil, Barbara Neill, with the long beard on him, and the horns above. Didn't you ever hear tell of the goats and the sheep?
1ST GIRL: Let you not be talking bad this day, Kitty Brien. Haven't you every day to do that? (IV. 288–9)

Both groups of children see the world in terms of symbols. The tinker children, fascinated by the 'green man' figure, however, are practical rather than speculative; they talk of a fertility symbol without questioning its significance, but eager to exploit its money-making possibilities. The village children, however, approach the notion of diabolical goats and submissive sheep with superstitious prurience. Moreover, they regard their religion as purely a matter for Sundays whereas the 'pagan' tinkers allow their dreams to suffuse every day of their lives.

Synge cut the children out of the final version of his play. It may seem, therefore, absurd to spend so much time discussing them. These passages, however, indicate themes in which Synge was interested, and enable us to see that, although he cut them out in the interests of dramatic economy, he retained their themes, and presented them in a more subtle manner.

The play was originally called *Movements of May*, a month for which Synge appears to have had a particular fondness, to judge from his many references to it. The awakening of the year is given mythic overtones and linked with the emotional excitement of Sarah Casey. At the beginning of the play Michael asks her: 'Can't you speak a word when I'm asking what is it ails you since the moon did change?' Her reply includes the statement 'spring-time is a queer time, and it's queer thoughts maybe I do think at whiles' (IV. 7). Her queer thoughts include a fancy that she has 'a right' to be going off 'to the rich tinkers do be travelling from Tibradden to the Tara Hill' (IV. 9). Although the phrase 'have a right to' is an Irish locution meaning, quite simply, 'should' or 'ought', Synge utilizes its potential ambiguity here as he did that of the word 'destroyed' in *Riders to the Sea*. Sarah's 'right' is, of course, the right of any unmarried woman to choose her own male companions, and her words contain a threat which frightens Michael. They also, however, remind us that Tara Hill is the most royal place of Irish legend, its religious and secular capital. Later Sarah expresses her admiration for Jaunting Jim who sold a 'white foal' for 'gold' and has a 'grand eye for a fine horse, and a grand eye for a woman' (IV. 11). White horses are commonly associated with both royalty and faerie. It is clear that, as Michael says, Sarah is 'easy pleased with a big word' (IV. 11). She refers to herself with pride as the 'Beauty of Ballinacree' (IV. 11). The consequences of her beauty are, however, less heroic than her pride in them might suggest. She boasts of the 'peelers' following her for ten miles and 'talking love' (IV. 11) and of the way the children are awed by her beauty. In an earlier version of the play she also talks of the admiration of a gentleman and of young ladies by the sea-shore 'running this way and that way . . . trying would they sketch my face and I letting on I wouldn't see them at all . . . ' (IV. 10). Disturbed by the 'change of the moon' at the time of the vernal equinox, she is filled with a rising excitement and sense of her own royal beauty, and expresses this in language that conflates folk-tale and ancient belief with the commonplace. She is being carried along upon one of the 'movements of May'.

If Sarah Casey, in her excited language, provides us with that dimension of ancient belief which was provided in other drafts by the 'green man' passage, all the characters in combination indicate the cultural cross-currents involved in those 'movements'. Sarah refers to Mary as a 'divil's scholar' (IV. 29) likely to turn the priest against them. Michael says 'it's the divil's job making a ring' (IV. 7). Mary combines in her outlook the pagan and the ostensibly Christian. She tells her companions that she has 'a grand story of the great queens of Ireland with white necks on them the like of Sarah Casey, and fine arms would hit you a slap the way Sarah Casey would hit you' (IV. 25). When Michael and Sarah refuse to stay and listen to her story, but leave her alone with no money for drink, she cries:

What good am I this night, God help me? What good are the grand stories I have when it's few would listen to an old woman, few but a girl maybe would be in great fear her hour was come, or a little child wouldn't be sleeping with the hunger on a cold night? (IV. 27)

The psychic energy which gives rise to dreams of splendour also gives rise to violence of speech and action, as we saw in the passage in which the little girls dressed for confirmation comment upon and are themselves commented upon by the tinkers. In the first act, though Sarah occasionally allows her vehemence full play, she is dominated by her desire for marriage. In the second act, when all her wheedlings fail to move the priest who is insistent upon receiving as part of his fee the tin can he has been promised, and which has been sold for drink by Mary, she becomes violent, first threatening to attack Mary, and then shouting at the priest, who attempts to intervene.

I've bet a power of strong lads east and west through the world, and are you thinking I'd turn back from a priest? Leave the road now, or maybe I would strike yourself. (IV. 43)

A little later, when the priest threatens to tell the police who stole Philly O'Cullen's ass, her love of language leads her to a superbly absurd vision.

If you do, you'll be getting all the tinkers from Wicklow and Wexford, and the County Meath, to put up block tin in the place of glass to shield your windows where you do be looking out and blinking at the girls. It's hard set you'll be that time, I'm telling you, to fill the depth of your belly the long days of Lent; for we wouldn't leave a laying pullet in your yard at all. (IV. 45)

The same wildness of imagination is shown by Mary, whose speeches move easily from the idealistic to the bawdy, but at the close of the play it is Sarah and not Mary who suggests that if the police arrive the priest should be thrust 'headfirst in the boghole is behind the ditch' (IV. 45).

The wildness and savagery of Sarah Casey is, it is emphasized, not simply the consequence of her cultural inheritance, her coming of a breed without the law, but also of the 'change of the moon'. Mary makes the point twice. In the first act she says to Michael: 'Didn't you hear me telling you she's flighty a while back since the change of the moon?' (IV. 23); and in the second she says 'Oh! isn't she a terror since the moon did change' (IV. 31). This is not intended to exculpate Sarah entirely; it is, however, intended to suggest that those wandering folk who live in close proximity to the natural world, a proximity and familiarity emphasized many times in the play, can be affected by the seasonal changes in their environment. Like the people in *Riders to the Sea* and *The Shadow of the Glen*, Sarah Casey is the victim of the elements, and yet also is 'in harmony with some mood of the earth'. It is the quickening of May that has influenced Sarah Casey. The unfixed nature of her life has made her free of moralities we associate with the ownership and protection of property, and given her, at this time of emotional hunger, a yearning for the greatest novelty she could experience, that of becoming part of an established moral and social order. May, however, will pass and Mary Byrne shows her understanding of Sarah's predicament by talking of the future. A wedding ring will not stop Sarah growing old or ease her pains, she informs her, and Sarah is, for a moment, doubtful. Later, talking to the priest in his bag, Mary says:

It's sick and sorry we are to tease you; but what did you want meddling with the like of us, when it's a long time we are going our own ways – father and son, and his son after him, or mother and daughter, and her own daughter again – and it's little need we ever had of going up into a church and swearing – I'm told there's swearing with it – a word no man would believe, or with drawing rings on our fingers, would be cutting our skins maybe when we'd be taking the ass from the shafts, and pulling the straps the time they'd be slippy with going around beneath the heavens in rains falling. (IV. 47)

This speech is, in effect, the final version of the speech about the pigs and the rings in their noses which appeared in the very first draft of the play that Synge made in 1902. The tone is calmer. Mary is not without sympathy for the priest's predicament, and addresses him as 'good boy' as well as 'holy father' and 'your reverence'. She chides rather than hectors. And yet the philosophy she presents has not altered a whit, though four years passed between the writing of the first version and the final touches being made to the last draft; the softening down has not changed the message.

This particular message may be one of the reasons that Synge himself described his play as thought 'too immoral' for production. He also reported that it was considered 'anti-clerical'. The figure of the priest, however, is by no means completely absurd. In the first draft of the play he is little more than a cardboard cut-out. In the second he is described as 'fat' and is bad-tempered and arrogant throughout his appearance. When Synge expanded the play from one act to two, however, he gave the priest more material and more character. Though described by

Sarah as 'a big boast of a man with a long step on him and a trumpeting voice' (IV. 13) he shows some sympathy for the tinkers. At first inclined to scorn them entirely, and to dismiss their request for marriage by demanding additional payments he must know to be impossible, he is puzzled and touched by Sarah's weeping with disappointment. 'Let you not be crying, Sarah Casey,' he tells her. 'It's a queer woman you are to be crying at the like of that, and you your whole life walking the roads' (IV. 15). He shows brusque concern for the drunken Mary, warning her when she appears in danger of falling in the fire, and good humouredly shares her porter. He relaxes in the friendly atmosphere and complains of his 'hard life' and his fear of the bishop 'coming in the morning, and he an old man would have you destroyed if he seen a thing at all' (IV. 19). He is not, however, a hypocrite. He is honestly scandalized by Mary's telling him she had never heard a prayer, and when she drunkenly catches hold of him and insists that he say one, he breaks away from her, saying, 'Leave me go, Mary Byrne; for I never met your like for hard abominations the score and two years I'm living in the place,' and then adds, after a little space, 'God have mercy on your soul' (IV. 21).

The priest is, indeed, a reasonably friendly man, fully aware of the tinkers' characters but willing to take a chance on Sarah's change of heart. His insistence upon getting 'the bit of gold' and the tin can, 'though it's a pitiful small sum' (IV. 23), may be less avarice than a desire to ensure that the tinkers take the whole affair seriously. He is 'half terrified' at the violence of Mary Byrne's language in the second act, and thinks it might be a 'queer job' to give Christian sacrament to her kind, and, perhaps a little nervously, offers a shilling to them to forget the whole idea. Even at this point, however, he is susceptible to persuasion and when Sarah says that she will complain to the bishop if he does not keep his word, he is first astonished and then moved by her passionate assertion that she would do it 'if I walked to the city of Dublin with blood and blisters on my naked feet' (IV. 33). The image conjures up, of course, thoughts of pilgrimages and of ascetics. Again he agrees to perform the ceremony, saying:

77

I wish this day was done, Sarah Casey; for I'm thinking it's a risky thing getting mixed in any matters with the like of you.   (IV. 33)

One can hardly blame him for his anger when the tinkers fail to keep their end of the bargain, or for his agreeing not to inform on them when he is tied in a bag and in real danger of his life. Nor can one do anything but admire the resourcefulness and humour he shows at the close of the play by trumpeting out his unintelligible Latin to set them all running off in fear of damnation.

Why then was the play thought anti-clerical? Daniel Corkery, the play's most violent critic, wrote that 'no one reared in an Irish Catholic household would dream of creating a similar figure, unless of course, he were, like Liam O'Flaherty, a mere sensationalist', and saw him as 'ludicrous'.[6] He felt the priest was so untypical as to be invalid as a dramatic character. He might have been on firmer ground had he noticed that it is not the priest, but Mary Byrne, who understands exactly what motivates Sarah. The priest may be a man long experienced in human follies, but he is not as close to the 'movements' of the human heart as the drunken old tinker woman who embodies both the folly and the wisdom of the play. He is as out of touch with the reality of human emotion as the priest in *Riders to the Sea*. His view of life is simplistic, naïve, and he shows no spirituality at all. He has, however, for all his blusterings, a kind of endearing innocence, and an optimistic heart, which make him far more sympathetic as a character than Michael, who is very much the victim of the situation. Both the men, in fact, are baffled by the women. Both are driven to make decisions they mistrust. And while both triumph in the end, the priest sending the tinkers running and Michael gloating over his gold and able to contemplate 'drinking that bit with the trampers on the green of Clash' (IV. 49), it is the women who have dominated the whole episode and who, one feels, will master whatever situation they encounter, for their psychic vitality is such as to persuade all comers that their vision of life is desirable.

The Tinker's Wedding is not Synge's greatest play, though it is his most 'rollicking'. It is hard to sympathize with Corkery's sorrow that 'Synge ever wrote so poor a thing', though it is easy to see why the 'wilful nationalism' of the Ireland of his time would find it unacceptable. Synge was struggling to present a vision of humanity trapped by 'the movements of May', and also attempting to say something at once true in its particulars and profound in its general implications of the nature of a rootlessness attended with traditional beliefs and attitudes when it comes up against conventional, rooted, property-owning society. The ancient and the new clash in this small, and in some ways Chaucerian, tale, which shows, as Boccaccio shows in similar stories, the conflict of conventional religious practice with wildness of heart and passionate hungers. Synge wrote as early as 1899 in a review of a book by Anatole le Braz published in the *Daily Express* (Dublin) of that year, words which may refer to his Aran experiences but which also apply to *The Tinker's Wedding*:

Here, again, lies one great interest of this movement of the Celtic races, for whenever the two streams of humanity – the old and the new – flow for but a moment side by side, blending old attachments with new indomitable joys, this moment grows rich with a pregnant luxuriance undreamed of hitherto, and from moments such as these depend the purer movements of mankind.   (II. 394)

The Tinker's Wedding was not produced until after Synge's death. In 1909 it was played by the Afternoon Theatre Company at His Majesty's Theatre, London, on 11 November, and was not a success, seeming to *The Times* reviewer, 'less a play than a picture of Irish life in its more squalid aspects'. Sixty years later, in 1969, when we are observing among the young a multitude of rootless people obeying no law but that of their imaginations, their ideals and their rejection of bourgeois conventions of property and morality, some of them even emulating, in their music and their poetry, the romantic and high-sounding dreams of Sarah Casey and Mary Byrne, *The Tinker's Wedding* does not seem quite so easy a play to dismiss. Indeed, in *The Tinker's Wedding*, the third of his shanachie plays, Synge chose by means of rollicking farce to present a conflict that has become in the ensuing years ever more central to our Western society.

CHAPTER SEVEN

Verse Plays

Although Synge never completed a play in verse to his own satisfaction he tackled several and, in sorting out his manuscripts
before his death, preserved enough of three of them to allow
us to get some idea of his work in this field. These three are
A Vernal Play whose first draft was completed on 27 March 1902,
and which appears to have been revised in January 1903,
Luasnad, Capa and Laine which appears to have been begun in
March 1902 and to have reached the revision stage in January
1903, and *The Lady O'Connor* which he worked on in 1903 and
1904, and which, in September 1904, he considered recasting in
prose.

A Vernal Play is written in iambic pentameter and is for the
most part in rhyming couplets. The plot, so far as one can
deduce it from the two fragments remaining, is slight. Cermuid
and his wife Boinn meet two girls, Etain and Niave, in a wood
near Glen Cree. The girls are out to pick flowers and 'meet
the Glen Cree shepherds' (III. 189). After some conversation
an Old Man enters and talks with them. He is the oldest man in
the glen and says he is 'friend of love' (III. 191). The first scene
breaks off shortly after this. The second scene reveals that the
Old Man has died, and Boinn, Etain, and Niave chant a 'death-
rhyme' over him. The fragment ends with Boinn and Cermuid
reasserting their love for one another.

There are no profound messages here. The whole piece
appears to be simply an attempt to express a lyrical mood and
show how it is possible to accept and revere both youth and age,
death and love. The tone is level and the speeches are leisurely.

Even the keen is without angularity or roughness. The poetry, however, reveals some interesting things. Firstly, it includes much more colloquial speech than is to be found in any other verse drama of this period with the exception of that of John Davidson. Certainly Synge is attempting to forge a language which can escape the defects of late Victorian blank-verse and make use of native Irish speech. Thus we have Boinn saying:

> Sycamores
> And larch and birch and sallows breathe new stores
> The time the rain is falling and it warm
> The way it's falling this day.　　　　　　　　　(III. 190)

This may not be great dramatic utterance; for one thing the phrase 'breathe new stores' is literary and conventional and thus contrasts rather clumsily with the following colloquialism, and for another the colloquialism itself lacks easy authority. Nevertheless the attempt is interesting.

In this play Synge also attempted to give strength to his speech by using specific references to place. Thus we have references to Glen Cree, Clash, Drumnamoe, Glenasmoil, Killnahole, Kilmashogue, Glen Dubh, Glencullen and Slieve Ruadh. The names are used for euphony as well as to emphasize the intensity of the characters' feelings about their familiar countryside.

The keen is almost epigrammatic. The four couplets are chanted in turn by Etain, Boinn, Niave, and Boinn again:

> All young girls must yield to rage,
> All firm youth must end in age.
>
> I call the lambs that browse with fright
> To mourn the man who died tonight.
>
> Every eye must fade and blear,
> Every bone bleach bare and clear.
>
> All must rise from earth and clay,
> All must end in green decay.　　　　　　　　　(III. 192)

Although there are elements of toughness in this play, there are also elements of the dreaminess we associate with the romantic verse drama of the time and with the early work of Yeats.

81

> Across Slieve Ruadh all the hills have wrapt
> New blueness from the raining. Hills as these
> Young men in dreams have walked on.   (III. 192)

The mood is contemplative, almost drowsy, and the love of natural beauty is expressed in melancholy cadences even though the statements may be of joy.

There is a little of Synge's originality here, but only a little. There is more in *Luasnad, Capa and Laine*, where the language is stronger, harder, and the theme one which Synge utilized in many of his writings. He took the basic idea from Geoffrey Keating's *The History of Ireland* which he first read in September 1900. In 1902 he reviewed for *The Speaker* David Comyn's English translation of Keating's first volume, in which the story of Capa, Laighne, and Luasad (Comyn's spellings) is told. It runs:

Some others say that it is three fishermen who were driven by a storm of wind from Spain unwillingly; and as the island pleased them that they returned for their wives to Spain; and having come back to Ireland again, the deluge was showered upon them at Tuaigh Innbir, so that they were drowned: Capa, Laighne, and Luasad, their names. It is about them the verse was sung:

> Capa, Laighne, and Luasad pleasant,
> They were a year before the deluge
> On the island of Banbha of the bays;
> They were eminently brave.   (III. 194)

From this Synge elaborated a short verse drama filled with savage awareness of approaching doom. Luasnad and Capa are talking hopefully of the rains ceasing when there is a cry of women's voices.

> CAPA: Your wife is still in labour?
> LUASNAD: When women do good things they choose a time
> That makes it silly. Here the child will die.   (III. 196)

The down-to-earth word 'silly' is shocking in this atmosphere of cosmic upheaval, and the whole statement is brutal. Laine joins the other two and they attempt to work out how fast the flood is rising and if it is likely to stop. Laine suggests picking up stones to kill the hares:

> Pick stones Capa, the hares are hid so thick
> Above us in the heather they will starve
> And if they starve we perish. (III. 196)

Capa says hopefully:

> All the goats
> Will swim straight over from the eastern peak
> For it will soon be covered. (III. 196)

The primitive nature of the men's viewpoints and the simplicity of their needs is indicated here cleanly and unrhetorically. The physical elements of the scene are impressed on us. Capa says:

> Something moves across the red-gold pathway.
> Look on it Laine, I have looked so long
> I see green moons about me. (III. 197)

The image is at once hallucinatory in its intensity and yet entirely intelligible in terms of common experience. The images in this play are all clearly and cleanly derived from common experience and none is inappropriate to the simplicity of these men. Thus Capa suggests that the moving object may be:

> . . . the curagh
> That we first came from Spain in, for the prow
> Is bending backward like a man's closed hand. (III. 197)

Again the image is both simple and graphic. Only when it becomes certain that the boat will not reach them does Luasnad cry, in phrases reminiscent of *King Lear*:

> The gods but toy
> And make their sport to urge our sightless hope. (III. 197)

Hope of another kind then arrives, for there is the cry of a child. This spark of new life, however, is doomed to die out, as we are told in an exchange of monosyllabic simplicity and strength:

> LAINE: Your child is born Luasnad, and it lives.
> CAPA: It is the first man's child has cried on Banba.
> LUASNAD: It will be the first dead human body.
> Count the hills.
> LAINE: Lugdubh,
> Craigmoira, Tonagee and Inchavor.
> LUASNAD: Three are covered?
> LAINE: And the rest are sinking. (III. 197)

83

Laine expresses a belief that the goats will swim to their island and their milk will feed the boy. The wife of Capa reports that the new mother has died. The goats swim past. Laine falls into the rising water and is deluded into thinking it fresh. Luasnad watches him and Capa drinks and says bitterly: 'The gods are jesting with them' (III. 198).

Still they attempt to hope. The corpse of Luasnad's wife is brought in and the other two women keen over her. It is now that Luasnad begins to develop his philosophy of despair:

> WIFE OF LAINE: Is there a war among the gods and have
> The sea gods conquered?
> LUASNAD:　　　　　　　There is no war.
> The gods work only to gain peace from prayer.　　　(III. 200)

Luasnad's vision of the gods wearied by man's appeals and complaints is a sombre one, but as the play continues and the child dies and all but he and the wife of Laine are drowned his picture becomes even more terrible:

> All this life has been a hurtful game
> Played out by steps of anguish. Every beast
> Is bred with fearful torment in the womb
> And bred by fearful torments in life-blood.
> Yet by a bait of love the aimless gods
> Have made us multitudes.　　　　　　　　　(III. 200)

The word 'bait' is brutal in its implications. We are lured by love into suffering, and love is no more than a lure. The gods are malicious as well as aimless. Laine's wife emphasizes the insignificance of human life to the gods when she describes how all the others were washed out to sea:

> ... As I climbed toward them came a wave
> Curling across the boulders where they sat
> That took them all as I would take some feathers
> And threw them out to sea.　　　　　　　　(III. 201)

Luasnad believes that if the gods have any aim it is to destroy man and replace him with:

> ... a new race more fit
> Than man has been to bear the rage of life.　　　(III. 202)

He sees their lives as being like:

> These crowns of foam that gleam and flash with gold
> And when our storm of passion has died out
> A few old gods will just remember man.   (III. 202)

Later when Laine's wife has complained bitterly of being about to die so young, and expressed a faint hope that maybe the gods will take pity on her, Luasnad, holding her in his arms, says:

> The gods have never made us. They have gotten
> Our first grey seed upon the slime of earth
> And have dealt with us as we deal with kine
> Who know the one brother. We are one
> With all this moon and sea white and the wind
> That slays us. And our passions move when we die
> Among the stars that wander or stand quiet
> In the great depths of night.

> WIFE OF LAINE: Take your hand
> Down from my bosom Luasnad.   (III. 203)

The introduction, thus simply and strongly, of rising physical desire after the imagery of grey seed and slime is both powerful and disturbing. Man and woman, left alone to face destruction, cling to one another in passion, and lust is a last challenge to the fates:

> LUASNAD: You the fairest of all women, turn your lips.
> The last strong man must perish,
> Let me flash a last red flame of love
> Across the brink of death, and shout defiance
> Up to the aimless gods.   (III. 204)

Later, when Laine's wife remembers her dead husband, Luasnad says:

> Dead men pass. There lives
> One only life, one passion of one love,
> One world wind sea, then one deep dream of death.

And:

> Man's last high mood
> Can pass above this passion of the seas
> That moans to crush him. In each man's proper joy
> The first high puissance that made live the gods
> Lives on the earth and asks the stone for worship.   (III. 205)

The play, as we now have it ends:

> LUASNAD: Heed not the gods. In this high passionate sea
> Mere gods would perish—
> WIFE OF LAINE: Ah! See the dark black vessel.
>
> *They are swept off.*   (III. 205)

The text that we have of this drama is certainly not one which Synge considered final. It is made up of, to quote Dr Saddlemyer who reconstructed it, 'twenty-four hastily scribbled and heavily amended manuscript pages', in a notebook from which some pages have been torn out. Nevertheless the play is a coherent and moving whole. The imagery is powerful and some of Luasnad's speeches have Shakespearean authority and muscularity. Though the tension of the play depends largely upon a movement between hope and despair rather than upon any character conflict, there is some conflict of loyalties in Laine's wife as she feels the rising passion to procreate which, Luasnad suggests, must disturb any whole being facing imminent death; the remainder of the characters, however, are only puppets. This is proper, for the play regards man as little more than a victim of an aimless though powerful force which shapes and shakes the whole world, making little distinction between wave and woman, man or mountain. The passionate cries in the face of death are typical of Synge and of the peasantry he observed in Aran. The boldness of his presentation of sexual needs in extremity can hardly be overstated when one considers the time at which the play was written. *Luasnad, Capa and Laine* is not perhaps a stageable play, but like Byron's *Manfred* and *Cain*, it is a powerful piece of closet drama and a good deal more direct, vivid and disturbing than most specimens of this.

There is one other specimen of closet drama which must be mentioned here, however. This is Yeats' *The Shadowy Waters*, which was first published in 1900 and later much revised. In this dramatic poem we have, as in *Luasnad, Capa and Laine*, much talk of the gods, and in a setting also dominated by the sea, and there are some interesting parallels. Forgael says:

> In the eyes of the gods
> War-laden galleys, and armies on white roads,

And unforgotten names, and the cold stars
That have built all are dust on a moth's wing.
They are their lures, but they have set their hearts
On tears and laughter; they have lured you hither
And lured me hither, that you might be my love . . .[7]

Later Dectora says:

The gods weave nets, and take us in their nets,
And none knows wherefore; but the heart's desire
Is this poor body that reddens and grows pale.[8]

The image of the gods trapping man runs through *The Shadowy Waters*. Dectora is, she tells us, 'new to love' just as Laine's wife tells us, 'I am young. And I have never yet conceived with child' (III. 203). Forgael refers to love as 'imperishable fire': Luasnad speaks of 'a last red flame of love' (III. 204).

I am not suggesting that Synge was deliberately utilizing Yeats, but it seems possible that in writing both his verse plays of 1902–3 he had *The Shadowy Waters* in the back of his mind. *A Vernal Play* ends:

BOINN: What fragrance, twist it in my hair that I
Through all the night may dream of flowery hills

While he crowns her she throws her arms round him.

Oh, Man, I would live ever lone with you,
Where every bough and hill-turn breathes with joy.

When they are gone for a little time two carrion crows come down and perch on the rock above the OLD MAN.

The Shadowy Waters (1900) ends with Dectora crowning Forgael:

DECTORA: I crown you with this crown.

She kneels beside him and puts her arms about him.

Bend lower, O King,
O flower of the branch, O bird among the leaves,
O silver fish that my two hands have taken
Out of a running stream, O morning star
Trembling in the blue heavens like a white fawn
Upon the misty border of the wood, –
Bend lower, that I may cover you with my hair,
For we will gaze upon this world no longer.

The harp begins to murmur of itself.

87

FORGAEL: The harp-strings have begun to cry out to the eagles.[9]

The parallelism here is in three matters: the crowning, the embracing, the image of hair. The contrast is of course between the final images, one of carrion crows and one of eagles, and between Boinn's life-acceptance and Dectora's rejection of the real world.

All this may mean only that Synge, in using images which are, after all, not infrequent in poetry of the period, and in tackling themes of love, death, and desolation which, again, are not uncommon in the period after 1890, chose to handle them in a different way from Yeats, but could not avoid having some words in common with him, at least in the early unrevised drafts, which are all we have. There would, indeed, be no point in referring to these minor similarities were it not that similar parallelism occurs in other of Synge's and Yeats' works and therefore is inclined to make one suspect a degree of deliberate manipulation and, on the part of the drily humorous Synge, possibly a wish quietly to tease the unaware and less humorously inclined Yeats.

Whether or not this is the case with the two verse plays of 1902, the verse drama of 1903–4, *The Lady O'Connor*, presents no such possibilities. Based upon the story told Synge by Pat Dirane on Inishmaan in 1898, it exists only in fragments and its main interest is the vitality and drive of the verse which continually approaches light verse or even doggerel. It is usually in couplets, and many of these are clangorously rhymed, giving the statements an almost Byronic pertness and gaiety. Some of the rhymes are multi-syllable – Connor/honour, only/lonely, to her/fewer, Almighty/flighty – and these in combination with the directness of much of the language give the whole the same cut-and-thrust sprightliness that animates some rhyming passages in Elizabethan comedy.

DAN O'CONNOR: . . . And not let choose your wife?
O'CONNOR: Well? Who'd you choose?
DAN O'CONNOR: Moira Burke.
O'CONNOR: God help me, Dan, them screws
Would cheat the hide from living starving beasts
And have you broke with dowries paying priests –

And –
DAN O'CONNOR: Let you whisht, but leave me what you've there
And I'll soon settle.
O'CONNOR: Glory, will you swear
You'll not ask more all your living life?
DAN O'CONNOR: I swear by God and by my hope to wife! (III. 209–10)

This is very crude stuff. It does, however, suggest that Synge was looking for a verse form that could carry the rollicking and vivid dialogue which he used in some of his prose plays. He attempted in this play also to include a passage of wild fancy similar to those which are the product of Mary Byrne in *The Tinker's Wedding*:

LADY O'CONNOR: I'm thinking it's well for you all your life,
Walking the world while I, when the wet clouds lift
Look only all the day on the seas and clifts.
CAPTAIN: Yet you have silky pillows for your bed,
And golden combs, I'm thinking, comb your head,
It's roasted hares you'll eat and dearest wine,
And lay your feet on mats of Persian twine,
While we live shut in ships that roll and pitch,
We eating salt till our shin marrows itch.
And drinking filthy water from a barrel
Our crew half naked through their ripped apparel. . . .
LADY O'CONNOR: It's small good women get from wines or mats.
I'd liefer stray like tinkers through the flats
Leinster's Aluin, or the bogs of Meath,
Than sit reckoning up the sighs I breathe.
CAPTAIN: Your Lord's a gallous talker and with him –
LADY O'CONNOR: He's half monk –
CAPTAIN: Oh, ho!
LADY O'CONNOR: I say he'll skim
The goat's milk in the morning, eat the cream,
He talking all the while of Jacob's dream.
And when he takes a rag to skim his spoon
You'd think to hear him that he owned the moon.   (III. 212–13)

This passage in its anti-romantic vigour may remind one not only of various parodies and imitations of *The Passionate Shepherd* but also of Synge's own comments on preferring to 'Poach with Red Dan Sally's bitch' rather than contemplate 'the plumed yet skinny Shee' (I. 38). Once again the life of vigour, and, it seems, of sexual vigour, is preferred to that of passivity and contemplation. In this *The Lady O'Connor* differs from *A Vernal Play* very considerably. We might almost suggest that in *A Vernal Play* Synge was still using conventional attitudes and language while attempting to diversify them with colloquialism and concrete imagery, that in *Luasnad, Capa and Laine* he found a way to present epic dramatic situations in a bare, hard language that could rise naturally into rhetoric, but which was only appropriate for tragedy, and in *Lady O'Connor*, having escaped completely from the conventional stock attitudes of the drama of his period, he tackled the problem of vigorous and sardonic dramatic verse that should carry some of the quality of folk ballad and folk speech, and gallop along with as much vigour as the speeches of Nora Casey or Mary Byrne. He could not, however, solve his problem. The fragments we have are all somewhat crudely organized and even pantomimic. In 1904, therefore, he began to think of reworking the play in prose, and after a time gave it up to perfect the now complete draft of *The Well of the Saints*, which was burdened with a less cumbersome plot and which did, in fact, include a more thorough and persuasive attack upon those false values with which the scraps of *Lady O'Connor* indicate that he was concerned.

Synge was not a verse dramatist. Two of his surviving fragments are worth little. The third, however, *Luasnad, Capa and Laine*, does give us further insight into the death-obsessed and passionate imagination of the man who throughout his days found it impossible to bow to the gods so unthinkingly revered and admired by his countrymen, or to credit providence with anything more than aimless and ultimately destructive energy.

CHAPTER EIGHT

The Well of the Saints

Synge is generally supposed to have first become interested in the theme of a miraculous cure of the blind by coming across a holy well on his first visit to Aran in May 1898. In his notebooks there is a rough draft of the account which later appeared in *The Aran Islands*. This, omitting all scribbled revisions and second thoughts, reads:

At the church of St Carolan which I have just visited with my old guide there is a holy well remarkable for many cures. While we loitered in the neighbourhood an old man came to us from a near cottage and told us how it became famous. A woman of Sligo had one son who was blind. She dreaming of a well that held water potent to cure so she took boat with her son following the course of her dream and reached Aran. She came to the house of my informant's father and told what had brought ⌊her⌋ but when those around offered to lead her to the well nearby she declined all aid saying she saw still her way clear before [her]. She led her son from the [house] and going a little up the hill stopped at the well. Then kneeling with the blind child beside her she prayed [to] god and bathed his eyes. In [a] moment his face gleamed with joy as he said 'Oh Mother look at the beautiful flowers.' Twice since the same story has been told to me with unimportant variations yet ending always with the glad dramatic cry of the young child. (III. 263–4)

Synge rewrote this for publication in his book, and enlivened it with dialogue, but the story remains the same in all essentials save that the church is now described as 'an old ruined church of the Ceathair Aluinn (The Four Beautiful Persons)' (II. 56).

This may be the first time Synge wrote of a holy well. It cannot, however, have been the first time he ever heard of one, especially as he had, in France, spent much time studying folklore.

It was in France in the spring of 1895 and the winter of 1896–7 that he attended courses given at the Sorbonne by Professor Petit de Julleville, the author of *Histoire du Théâtre en France au Moyen-âge*. On 3 October 1903 he made notes of portions of Chapters II and III of the volume *La Comédie et les Mœurs au Moyen-âge* (1886). These chapters include a description of Andrieu de la Vigne's *Moralité de l'Aveugle et du Boiteux* (1456). It is clear that this is the 'early French farce' which Synge told Padraic Colum that *The Well of the Saints* had been inspired by. The story is simple. Greene and Stephens summarize it thus:

A blind man agrees to carry a crippled man on his back so that each can compensate for the other. The arrangement is completely successful until they are both cured by passing a procession in which the remains of St Martin are displayed. The blind man is delighted, but the cripple curses the saint for destroying an easy life on the back of his companion.[10]

Synge began work on the play itself in the winter of 1903. He completed it in spring 1904, though he continued to tinker with it even after its first production at the Abbey Theatre on 4 February 1905 and its publication in book form at that time.

It is not necessary to comment in any detail on the various drafts of this play, for the majority of the changes in each are matters of expression and details of presentation rather than alterations of key images and symbols. The general process of writing is the same as that of *The Tinker's Wedding*: continual adjustments of scale and refinements of speech, stage directions, and nuances. Synge was, in such matters, a perfectionist, but *The Well of the Saints* is the only one of his plays that received considerable amendment after its production and publication. This obviously points to his unease about it. It also, however, suggests that he was aware that in this play of all plays exactitude of speech was important.

The reason for this is easy to see. In *The Well of the Saints* the central two characters build up their sense of identity by means of conversation and daydream rather than by action. We do not have an object at the centre of the play, as we have the clothes at the centre of *Riders to the Sea* and the tin can at the centre of *The Tinker's Wedding*. We do not have the dramatic suspense and mystery of *The Shadow of the Glen*. The play, indeed, opens with two beggars entering, sitting down, and talking. During the greater part of the first act there is little movement. It was the more important for Synge, therefore, to establish exactly the finer details. Thus we have a multitude of interpretive directions. The characters are made to speak 'with mock irony', 'a little plaintively' 'Sharply again, scandalized', 'pensively', 'bitterly' (III. 73), 'Teasingly, but with good humour' (III. 71), 'sadly', 'with a begging voice' (III. 75), 'rather contemptuously' (III. 77). We are told that they are 'slightly piqued' (III. 75), 'huffed', 'interested' (III. 77), that they speak 'with excitement', 'with disappointment' (III. 79). We are given details of the smallest gestures. Mary Doul 'puts her hand to her face with a complacent gesture and smooths her hair back with her hands' (III. 73). Timmy is described as 'hot and breathless, wiping his face' (III. 77). All these directions, and more, occur in the first five pages of the Oxford edition, and the variant readings in the manuscripts as often concern these niceties as those of speech.

Synge was extremely aware of the necessity to give exact directions to the actors and producers of his plays, and in several of them he went so far as to indicate the precise visual effect he intended. Thus in *Riders to the Sea*, he described the old women 'kneeling down in front of the stage with red petticoats over their heads' (III. 21). In another version of the play he was even more explicit, describing them as 'kneeling down in front of the stage with their backs to the people, and the white waist-bands of the red petticoats they wear over their heads just seen from behind' (III. 20). In *The Shadow of the Glen* Dan is described as jumping 'out of the bed in queer white clothes' (III. 53). In *The Tinker's Wedding* there are also extremely detailed stage directions, and many of them are interpretive. *The Well of the Saints*, however, exceeds them all in the quantity and detailed nature of its directions.

This is not only because the play frequently lacks physical movement, but also because it is essentially a psychological drama, in which the alterations of attitude and mood provide the dramatic rhythm, rather than the events which stimulate these movements. Synge's own analysis of the structure of the play emphasizes this. We cannot be sure whether this hand-written plan was made during the composition of the play or as a series of notes for the production of it, but it indicates clearly that Synge saw his drama as a kinetic pattern, a dynamically organized structure of emotional movement, rather than as a simple dramatized fable which is what it might appear to be on the surface.

Analysis Well of Saints

Act I

1. Martin and Mary	Exposition of characters and psychics	
2. + Timmy		
crescendo narrative	comedy	
3. + girls		
current more		
Martin excitement		
4. + Saint		
5. minus Saint		
6. quarrel	tragic	

II	Timmy and Martin	comic
	no current	
	2. Martin and Molly	traPoetical
	Love current	

III	Martin and Mary
	current of reawakened
	interest
	2. plus crowd
	current
	to make Martin
	recured

(III. 264)

If the play is read with this plan in mind its structure becomes clear. The first act opens with Mary and Martin Doul talking together and we are soon shown that Martin believes Mary to be beautiful and Mary herself is vain of her supposed 'white beautiful skin' and 'yellow hair' (III. 71). Like Sarah Casey in *The Tinker's Wedding* she has given herself a title; 'you know

94

rightly,' she says 'it was "the beautiful dark woman" they did call me in Ballinatone' (III. 73), 'dark' meaning blind.

The central theme is here introduced. Martin Doul says 'a little plaintively':

I do be thinking in the long nights it'd be a grand thing if we could see ourselves for one hour, or a minute itself, the way we'd know surely we were the finest man and the finest woman, of the seven counties of the east . . . (*bitterly*) and then the seeing rabble below might be destroying their souls telling bad lies, and we'd never heed a thing they'd say.

MARY DOUL: If you weren't a big fool you wouldn't heed them this hour Martin Doul, for they're a bad lot those that have their sight, and they do have great joy, the time they do be seeing a grand thing, to let on they don't see it at all . . .   (III. 73)

One of the versions of *The Well of the Saints* is called *When the Blind See*. This suggests perhaps too directly the possibility of paradox. The physically blind may 'see' glories to which the seeing are blind, and physical sight may result in that love of material beauty that is spiritual darkness. This is certainly one of the play's themes, although it does not emerge fully until the third act, when Martin Doul replies to the saint's praise of the world's beauty by saying:

Isn't it finer sights ourselves had a while since and we sitting dark smelling the sweet beautiful smells do be rising in the warm nights and hearing the swift flying things racing in the air, till we'd be looking up in our own minds into a grand sky, and seeing lakes, and broadening rivers, and hills are waiting for the spade and plough.   (III. 141)

The response of one of the onlookers, Mat Simon, to this speech is to roar with laughter and say: 'It's songs he's making now, holy father.' Patch adds: 'It's mad he is,' and Molly Byrne calls him 'lazy' and 'not wishing to work'.

The 'song' element in the Douls is shown in the exposition passages of the first act, not only in the lyricism of their fantasies and their love of the ideal self-portrait, but also in Martin's opposing truth to beauty by saying of Molly Byrne: 'If it's lies she does be telling she's a sweet beautiful voice you'd never tire to be hearing' (III. 73). When Timmy the smith enters, the Doul's false paradise of the mind is offered the blessing of a 'real wonder' (III. 77). The Douls, faced with an as yet vague 'real wonder', immediately think of grotesque and gross excitements, the discovery of a still, the hanging of a thief. It is as if reality can only intrude upon them in terms of appetite and suffering. During the earlier conversation Mary says 'there's a power of villainy walking in the world' (III. 75), 'they're a bad lot those that have their sight' (III. 73). As soon as Timmy explains about the saint, and the play becomes filled with anticipation, the girls come in and we see in Molly Byrne that a beautiful voice, and a beautiful appearance, can be a mask upon a much less attractive spirit.

The vitality of the play at this point derives, as so often in Synge, from incongruity and dramatic irony. Martin Doul is given the saint's cloak, and Molly, described as acting 'recklessly' and 'laughing foolishly', says: 'Isn't that a fine looking saint, Timmy the smith?' (III. 85). This is ironic in that, as we soon discover, Martin Doul is as visionary a man as the saint, and, at the end of the play, a good deal less naïve and more practical about the method to retain his peace of mind and vision of beauty. Moreover, the saint is shown, even in this first act, to be as morally blind as Martin is physically, for he thinks 'young girls' are 'the cleanest holy people you'd see walking the world' (III. 83). At this report of Molly Byrne's Mary Doul 'sits down, laughing to herself' and says, 'Well, the saint's a simple fellow, and it's no lie' (III. 83).

Nevertheless, if the saint is deluded, so is Mary Doul. When Martin Doul thinks of the beauty of the young girls he will see when he is cured, she thinks it odd that he should be so interested in the 'skinny young-looking girls' when he is 'married with a woman he's heard called the wonder of the western world' (III. 87).

The saint himself is as complacently secure in his viewpoint as Mary Doul, and his advice to the crowd of onlookers is another piece of dramatic irony:

... you'd do well to be thinking on the way sin has brought blindness to the world, and to be saying a prayer for your own sakes against false prophets and heathens, and the words of women and smiths, and all knowledge that would soil the soul or the body of a man. (III. 91)

When Martin Doul is healed, however, it is his seeing that brings

him into the sin of anger, violence, and ingratitude, and soon we see him as both lecherous and lazy. Moreover, it was the lies of Timmy the smith and of the girls that, earlier, kept Martin and Mary in their false paradise and in amity. Once healed, Martin turns on Mary and cries 'there's no man would liefer be blind a hundred years, or a thousand itself, than to be looking on your like' (III. 99).

The act ends, as Synge's plan indicates, in pathos and in the 'tragic'. The last speech of the saint drives home the multiple irony of the situation. It reads in part:

> May the Lord who has given you sight send a little sense into your heads, the way it won't be on your two selves you'll be looking – on two pitiful sinners of the earth – but on the splendour of the Spirit of God, you'll see an odd time shining out through the big hills, and steep streams falling to the sea. For if it's on the like of that you do be thinking, you'll not be minding the faces of men, but you'll be saying prayers and great praises, till you'll be living the way the great saints do be living, with little but old sacks, and skin covering their bones. . . . (III. 101)

This describes exactly the condition of the Douls when blind. They gazed upon the beauties of their imagination, and worshipped what was most pleasant in the sounds and scents of the countryside, thinking nothing of their ragged condition, but only of their fancied beauty.

The second act opens in what Synge has called the 'comic' mood. Banished from his mental paradise, Martin Doul says:

> For it's a raw beastly day we do have each day, till I do be thinking it's well for the blind don't be seeing the like of them grey clouds driving on the hill, and don't be looking on people with their noses red, the like of your nose, and their eyes weeping, and watering, the like of your eyes, God help you, Timmy the smith. (III. 105)

Later the absurdity is emphasized by Timmy:

> But it's a queer thing the way yourself and Mary Doul are after setting every person in this place, and up beyond to Rathvanna, talking of nothing, and thinking of nothing, but the way they do be looking in the face. It's the devil's work you're after doing with your talk of fine looks . . . (III. 111)

That which had validity in the world of imagination is disruptive in the world of fact. The creation of beauty from reality may be admirable, but the seeking of beauty in reality and the hungering

97

after it may be disruptive. This point is brought out by the next movement in the drama which Synge labels 'traPoetical' (meaning, presumably, to suggest the traditional poeticism of romantic rhetoric), and in which Martin Doul attempts to seduce Molly Byrne. After complaining of the ugliness of the world he says:

> . . but there's one fine thing we have, to be looking on a grand, white, handsome girl, the like of you . . . and every time I set my eyes on you I do be blessing the saints, and the holy water, and the power of the Lord Almighty in the heavens above. (III. 111)

His admiration of Molly occurs at the moment when his sight is beginning to darken again and he to return to his earlier way of dreaming. He talks of the 'great joy' he had in hearing her voice when he was blind, and how, when lying 'in a little rickety shed' thinking of her and hearing her, his imagination set him in a 'high room with timber lining the roof' (III. 113). Even now, however, while trying to persuade the girl to live with him, he says:

> . . . it's better I am, I'm thinking, lying down the way a blind man does be lying, than to be sitting here in the grey light, taking hard words of Timmy the smith. (III. 113–15)

Later he says:

> I'm thinking by the mercy of God it's few sees anything but them is blind for a space. It's few sees the old women rotting for the grave, and it's few sees the like of yourself, though it's shining you are, like a high lamp, would drag in the ships out of the sea. (III. 117)

Molly is 'half-mesmerized' by the poetic intensity of Martin's admiration. He tells her:

> . . . I'm seeing you this day, seeing you, maybe, the way no man has seen you in the world. (III. 117)

and takes her by the arm. Molly wakes from her coma, and firmly rejects him. When Mary Doul appears he begs Molly not to tell her what has happened:

> Let you not put shame on me and I after saying fine words to you, and dreaming . . . dreams . . . in the night. (III. 119)

The darkness is now descending upon him again, but before

the end of the act he curses Molly and Timmy, crying:

And that's the last thing I'm to set my sight on in the life of the world, the villainy of a woman and the bloody strength of a man.   (III. 123)

The dream of perfection which is possible to the blind cannot be sustained in the world of reality. The intensity of feeling which is created by the words of poetry frightens others, or mesmerizes them, but it does not change them. Timmy the smith may say, 'Oh, God protect us, Molly, from the words of the blind' (III. 121), but he is not asking protection from curses only, but from the strange and vivid light those words shed upon human affairs. He sees that the dream is a dangerous thing to all, including the dreamer if he should once be awoken.

The third act finds Mary and Martin Doul remaking their dream. Martin curses Mary Doul for 'putting lies on me, and letting on she was grand' (III. 125), but he also curses the saint 'for letting me see it was lies'. It is only when Mary Doul offers him her new dream of an old woman with 'soft white hair' (III. 129) and he creates his own vision of himself with 'a beautiful, long, white, silken streamy beard' (III. 131) that he regains his peace of mind. The two of them play happily with their new toys until they hear the bell of the saint, when Mary cries out in horror:

The Lord protect us from the saints of God!   (III. 133)

Frenziedly they attempt to think of a way of putting themselves beyond the saint's power. Then crouched in fear they try to hide from him.

MARY DOUL: Let you not be whispering sin, Martin Doul, or maybe it's the finger of God they'd see pointing to ourselves.
MARTIN DOUL: It's yourself is speaking madness, Mary Doul, haven't you heard the saint say it's the wicked do be blind?
MARY DOUL: If it is you'd have a right to speak a big terrible word would make the water not cure us at all.
MARTIN DOUL: What way would I find a big terrible word, and I shook with the fear, and if I did itself, who'd know rightly if it's good words or bad would save us this day from himself?   (III. 135)

This, both comic and pathetic, points to the central concern of the play. When the value systems of men are in conflict with each other, then the imposing of 'blessings' by one group upon another may result in hardship and confusion of mind. The idle dreamer, blind to reality, has his function as a source of entertainment to the realists, and may even give them opportunities for charity and sympathy, while himself feeling secure in a world which is no less truly delusory than that of others. Mary Doul may be uglier physically than she believes herself to be, but Molly Byrne is not the goddess-like creature she appears. The blind may father false appearances upon reality by creating fantasies based upon hearing only. The seeing may be equally deluded by placing too great a reliance upon appearances. The 'do-gooder' may do evil by bringing new problems into lives that were previously under-privileged but harmonious.

This is one of the 'essentials' Synge sought to present by means of his 'attributes'. He also, however, once again emphasized that man does not live by bread alone, and that it is the passionate heart which gives men dignity, rather than the rational intelligence. *The Well of the Saints* ends in triumph for the Douls. Martin spills the holy water and he and Mary set off for the south, undeterred by warnings that they will find the road hard and may die on the way. They would rather suffer physical privation than lose their dream. In this they are like the ideal Christian described by the saint. Their dream may not be as profound or glorious as that of the dedicated Christian, but it is the only one they have been able to create. It is, they feel, their inalienable right to have that dream. As Martin says:

We're going surely, for if it's a right some of you have to be working and sweating the like of Timmy the smith, and a right some of you have to be fasting and praying and talking holy talk the like of yourself, I'm thinking it's a good right ourselves have to be sitting blind, hearing a soft wind turning round the little leaves of the spring and feeling the sun, and we not tormenting our souls with the sight of the grey days, and the holy men, and the dirty feet is trampling the world. (III. 149)

It is the right, Martin suggests, of every man to choose his own way of life, however odd it may appear to others. He has a right not to bow down to conventional notions of the real or the important. He has a right to avoid 'tormenting' his 'soul'. Martin's view of the soul may not be theologically profound, but

Synge's view is interesting. From *The Well of the Saints*, as from *The Shadow of the Glen* and *The Tinker's Wedding*, it would seem that he took what we would now label an existentialist view. Existence precedes essence; it is the life-experience, including the experience of living traditions however flawed and gross, that gives each soul its individual character and its individual road to travel. The saint is an idealist, as are the priests in *The Tinker's Wedding* and *Riders to the Sea*, and as is the husband in *The Shadow of the Glen*: they believe that all must be forced into conformity with the Idea, the established order, the rule of morality and belief which pre-exists us all. Martin is not of this persuasion; nor is Synge. In every play he completed, with the possible exception of the first, he shows individuals asserting their 'right' to be 'blind' to realities that torment them and to protect and defend the vision that sustains their belief in their own human dignity, and in the perfectibility of their world. At the end of *The Well of the Saints* we see Timmy and Molly about to be married. Timmy says of the Douls:

There's a power of deep rivers with floods in them where you do have to be lepping the stones and you going to the south, so I'm thinking the two of them will be drowned together in a short while, surely.

The saint comments:

They have chosen their lot, and the Lord have mercy on their souls. . . . And let the two of you come now into the church, Molly Byrne and Timmy the smith, till I make your marriage and put my blessing on you all.

(III. 151)

The dubious value we now attach to the saint's blessing and our knowledge of Molly's flightiness must affect us at this point, and turn our minds to the Douls who have left together, secure in their vision, though in peril of their lives. *The Well of the Saints* is, of course, a fable and, like all fables, it preaches. It is also, however, so varied in mood, and so energetic in expression, that we find tragedy, comedy, and lyricism combining to give us a play with all the light and shade of the human condition. It expresses more distinctly than any other of Synge's plays his belief in individualism, his distrust of conventional idealism, his relish of those that stand up for their right to their vision. It may be no accident that Mary Doul calls herself the wonder of the western world, for she is, in her struggle to assert her dignity and in her fantasies of pride, kin to the playboy of the western world who also had a vision of his dignity and found it conflicting with the actual.

CHAPTER NINE

The Essays

Synge's essays and miscellaneous prose pieces can be divided into four groups. The first is that labelled 'The Man Himself' in Alan Price's edition of the Prose; it consists of those autobiographical and near-autobiographical pieces I have discussed at the beginning of this book. The second is that group of essays which Dr Price labels 'In Wicklow, West Kerry and Connemara'; this consists of essays and passages from notebooks dealing with Synge's experiences in the places named, and also a series of twelve articles commissioned by and published in the *Manchester Guardian*. The third group, which Dr Price gives the heading 'About Literature' consists of a scattering of notebook passages, a number of reviews, and Synge's previously unpublished 'Letter to the Gaelic League'. Apart from this letter the third group is interesting largely for its occasional general comments upon art, and many of these I have brought into play elsewhere in this book. It is the second group, indeed, that demands most attention. It is necessary, however, to subdivide it, for the essays are of two distinct kinds.

The first kind can briefly be summarized as essays written, like *The Aran Islands*, from Synge's own individual viewpoint and because he felt moved to write them. The second kind are essays written for the *Manchester Guardian* as a survey of the life in the depressed areas of Connemara and Mayo which were at that time receiving aid from the Congested Districts Board. Synge spent four weeks, with Jack Yeats as his companion, in these areas, and sent off three articles a week. Jack Yeats made drawings to accompany them. On 13 July 1905 Synge wrote to Stephen MacKenna:

... we had a wonderful journey, and as we had a purse to pull on we pushed into out-of-the-way corners in Mayo and Galway that were more strange and marvellous than anything I've dreamed of. Unluckily my commission was to write on the 'Distress' so I couldn't do anything like what I would have wished to do as an interpretation of the whole life. . . .[11]

W. B. Yeats, when going through Synge's manuscripts after his death, thought that these essays should not be reprinted, and because Maunsel insisted on including them in Volume IV of the 1910 edition of the Works, withdrew his preface from that book and published it separately as *J. M. Synge and the Ireland of his Time*. Certainly these essays lack those individual qualities which make the others so fascinating. What Synge might have written, had he been given a freer hand, is shown in his letter to MacKenna:

There are sides of all that western life the groggy-patriot-publican-general shop-man who is married to the priest's half-sister and is second cousin once-removed of the dispensary doctor, that are horrible and awful. This is the type that is running the present United Irish League anti-grazier campaign, while they're swindling the people themselves in a dozen ways and then buying out their holdings and packing off whole families to America. The subject is too big to go into here, but at best it's beastly. All that side of the matter of course I left untouched in my stuff. I sometimes wish to God I hadn't a soul and then I could give myself up to putting those lads on the stage. God, wouldn't they hop! In a way it is all heartrending, in one place the people are starving but wonderfully attractive and charming, and in another place where things are going well, one has a rampant, double-chinned vulgarity I haven't seen the like of.[12]

Although Synge did not attempt 'an interpretation of the whole life' in these essays, and forbore to give vent to his loathing of nepotism and chicanery, he did succeed in presenting levelly and lucidly the predicament of the peasants, and managed to include a number of those character-portraits in which he delighted. There is, however, nothing about the superstitions of the people; there are no expressions of intense feeling, and at a first reading one might believe Synge himself to have deliberately excised all elements of the picturesque and passionate. If one reads carefully, however, it is noticeable that strong feelings are implied. In visiting Spiddal he talks of the shopkeepers 'dressed like the people of Dublin, but a little more grotesquely' and the adverb has its effect, especially as at the end of the same sentence we read of the destitute 'patched and threadbare and ragged, the women mostly barefooted, and both sexes pinched with hunger and fear of it' (II. 287). The simple accounts of the situation given him by the peasants are moving because so devoid of explicit emotionalism. There is a weariness and lack of zest in their speech. Most of the talk is of practical matters, as if, in these straits, halfpence loomed so large as to block out other considerations. Criticism of social injustice is not lacking, but is played down, in keeping with the mood of resignation that dominates the people. We are told that the kelp buyer:

. . . takes a handful, tests it with certain chemicals, and fixes the price accordingly; but the people themselves have no means of knowing whether they are getting fair play, and although many buyers may be careful and conscientious, there is a very general feeling of dissatisfaction among the people with the way they are forced to carry on the trade.   (II. 309)

The word is 'many' and not 'most'; the implication is clear. Again after describing the way in which the Board has helped rebuild cottages, Synge talks of having visited one which, though renovated, still 'seemed natural and local' and adds, 'That at least was reassuring.' Again the words 'at least' provoke questions.

It is largely by means of such qualifying words and phrases that Synge builds up his picture. However, in the ninth article, that on Erris, he states openly:

The relief system, as it is now carried on, is an utterly degrading one. . . .
(II. 327)

In the tenth essay he tells us:

I asked a woman who had come in for a moment if she thought the girls kept their health in America.

'Many of them don't,' she said, 'working in factories with dirty air; and then you have likely seen that the girls in this place is big, stout people, and when they get over beyond they think they should be in the fashions, and they begin squeezing themselves in till you hear them gasping for breath, and that's no healthy way to be living.'   (II. 330)

This may be a comic picture, but it is also a bitter one. Synge emphasizes that the twin pressures of emigration and well-meaning but superficially thought-out reformation are slowly but surely destroying the cultural health of the West. In his last article, that on 'Possible Remedies', he suggests a number of practical solutions, including improved communications:

A good deal may be done also by improved communications, either by railroad or by sea, to make life easier for the people. For instance, before the steamer was put on a few years ago between Sligo and Belmullet, the cost of bringing a ton of meal or flour by road from Ballina to Belmullet was one pound, and one can easily estimate the consequent dearness of food. That is perhaps an extreme case, yet there are still a good many places where things are almost as bad, and in these places the people suffer doubly, as they are usually in the hands of one or two small shopkeepers, who can dictate the price of eggs and other small articles which they bring in to sell. (II. 340)

The practicality of his views in these essays is adjusted to his understanding of the people. He points out that the emigration problem is not a simple one. Some leave because there is no work. Where there is work, the earnings tempt others to buy their fares to America. Some leave poor districts reluctantly; others, in districts where there are entertainments, develop a taste for amusements and leave for that reason.

They go as much from districts where the political life has been allowed to stagnate as from districts where there has been an excess of agitation that has ended only in disappointment. For the present the Gaelic League is probably doing more than any other movement to check this terrible evil, and yet one fears that when the people realize in five, or perhaps in ten, years that this hope of restoring a lost language is a vain one the last result will be a new kind of hopelessness and many crowded ships leaving Queenstown and Galway. Happily in some places there is a counter-current of people returning from America. Yet they are not very numerous, and one feels that the only real remedy for emigration is the restoration of some national life to the people. It is this conviction that makes most Irish politicians scorn all merely economic or agricultural reforms, for if Home Rule would not of itself make a national life it would do more to make such a life possible than half a million creameries. (II. 341)

Yeats once said that Synge was 'unfitted to think a political thought'. He may have been correct in that Synge could never belong to any political organization without discomfort. He resigned from Maud Gonne's *Ireland Libre* movement shortly after joining it, because he wished to work for Ireland in his own fashion and did not feel he could do this if he were 'mixed up with a revolutionary and semi-military movement'.[13] Yeats was, however, wrong if he believed Synge incapable of thinking in terms of practical reform. Synge distrusted the Gaelic League's emphasis on a narrow nationalism as is shown in his intemperate 'Letter to the Gaelic League', which he headed, 'Can We Go Back Into Our Mother's Womb?' (II. 399–400). He felt that Irish was 'dying out year by year' as 'a living language', and that the League was 'founded on a doctrine that is made up of ignorance, fraud and hypocrisy'. He thought the movement 'gushing, cowardly and maudlin', and filled with 'the hysteria of old women's talk'. He says that he hopes someone will soon 'sweep over the backside of the world to the uttermost limbo this credo of mouthing gibberish', and makes it clear that the gibberish he refers to is the 'incoherent twaddle passed off as Irish' by the League and not the language of the old manuscripts or of the two or three dialects still spoken in the west and south. And, above all, he returns to his attack upon narrow and 'wilful nationalism' saying:

Was there ever a sight so piteous as an old and respectable people setting up the ideals of Fee-Gee because, with their eyes glued on John Bull's navel, they dare not be Europeans for fear the huckster across the street might call them English. (II. 400)

This was written in 1907. In 1902 in an article on 'The Old and New in Ireland', published in *The Academy and Literature* on 6 September, he made some of the same points more temperately. He suggested that the decay of Irish as a living language had, in fact, brought a new vigour to the writing of English by Irishmen.

With the present generation the linguistic atmosphere of Ireland has become definitely English enough, for the first time, to allow work to be done in English that is perfectly Irish in its essence, yet has sureness and purity of form. (II. 384)

He suggests that we should look at America:

The number of foreigners in America for whom English is a language they have either learned for themselves or picked up from parents who had learned it, tends more than anything else to cause the uncertainty of literary taste in that country . . . roughness of the spoken language – when it is not a primitive roughness – leads, or tends to lead, to burlesque writing, and with this in one's mind it is interesting to compare the school of Mark Twain with the crudely humorous 'typical Irishman', who was present everywhere in Irish writing till quite recently. (II. 385)

The 'national life' that Synge wishes to reinvigorate is described by implication in his other and more personal essays, in which he also, by example, shows how the English language may present something 'perfectly Irish in its essence'. These essays were written over the years 1898–1907, but as the later ones made use of early notebook materials there is no point in tackling them chronologically. The themes remain the same throughout, and include several of those dealt with extensively in *The Aran Islands*. Thus we have stories of the supernatural, comments upon the loneliness of the peasant life in the glens of Wicklow and the more desolate areas of Kerry, and continual indications of the closeness of life to the rhythms of the seasons and its inextricable involvement in the moods of nature – the melancholy of the rain, the sudden upsurge of vitality in the spring, the stoicism of wave-battered rocks, and the black imagery of the bogs.

There are, however, a number of other comments which show how Synge viewed the 'national life' which in his *Guardian* articles he felt should be preserved and reinvigorated. The national life he describes, however, appears to be one which no political reform could easily cope with, for its essence is freedom from the conventions we associate with twentieth-century urban-orientated normality. In an early note (1898) on a vagrant he wrote:

Man is naturally a nomad . . . and all wanderers have finer intellectual and physical perceptions than men who are condemned to local habitations. The cycle, automobile and conducted tours are half-conscious efforts to replace the charm of the stage coach and of pilgrimage like Chaucer's. But the vagrant, I think, along with perhaps the sailor has preserved the dignity of motion with its whole sensation of strange colours in the clouds and of strange passages with voices that whisper in the dark and still stranger inns and lodgings, affections and lonely songs that rest for a whole life time with the perfume of spring evenings or the first autumnal smoulder of the leaves. . . . There is something grandiose in a man who has forced all kingdoms of the earth to yield the tribute of his bread and who, at a hundred, begs on the wayside with the pride of an emperor. The slave and beggar are wiser than the man who works for recompense, for all our moments are divine and above all price though their sacrifice is paid with a measure of fine gold. Every industrious worker has sold his birthright for a mess of pottage, perhaps served him in chalices of gold. . . .   (II. 195–6)

This specimen of what Synge considers admirable in man is hardly one which could be approved of by capitalist democracy or bureaucratic socialism or, indeed, any political structure at present in the world. The last two sentences, indeed, adopt an attitude shared, fifty and sixty years after his death, by those young people that journalism has labelled hippies. They too believe that the way to keep each moment divine is to drop out from society and reject the golden bait, and they too are nomads who pass from strange lodging to strange lodging singing 'lonely songs'.

Synge is indeed as opposed to urban society as was Wordsworth, and for much the same reasons. In the peasants and nomads he finds 'people that unite in a rude way the old passions of the earth'. After meeting a beggar woman and encountering some tinker children he tells us in a notebook of 1901:

People like these, like the old woman and these two beautiful children, are a precious possession for any country. They console us, one moment at least, for the manifold and beautiful life we have all missed who have been born in modern Europe. . . .   (II. 199)

It is hard to think of a politician who would consider the country beggars, the tinkers and the gypsies, 'precious possessions' of his country – unless they were so picturesque as to attract the tourist trade. The word 'modern' here is significant, however. Though Synge has no sympathy with tyrannous landlords of the present or the past, and is passionately in sympathy with the starving and oppressed, he has yet a nostalgia for some of the values of a vanished aristocracy. He records how an old woman complained 'how lonely the country had become since the "quality" had gone away', and reports how an eighty-year-old man talked of the Synge family, and:

How a lady used to ride through Roundwood 'on a curious beast' to visit an uncle of hers in Roundwood Park, and how she married one of the Synge's and got her weight in gold – eight stone of gold – as her dowry: stories that referred to events which took place more than a hundred years ago. (II. 221)

This essay was published in 1907. In another on 'A Landlord's Garden in County Wicklow' published the same year he describes the boycotted house, Castle Kevin, where he spent his summer holidays as a boy, and talks of:

... the tragedy of the landlord class ... and of the innumerable old families that are quickly dwindling away. These owners of the land are not much pitied at the present day, or much deserving of pity; and yet one cannot quite forget that they are the descendants of what was at one time, in the eighteenth century, a high-spirited and highly-cultivated aristocracy. The broken green-houses and mouse-eaten libraries, that were designed and collected by men who voted with Grattan, are perhaps as mournful in the end as the four mud walls that are so often left in Wicklow as the only remnants of a farmhouse. ... Many of the descendants of these people have, of course, drifted into professional life in Dublin, or have gone abroad; yet, wherever they are, they do not equal their forefathers, and where men used to collect fine editions of *Don Quixote* and Molière, in Spanish and French, and luxuriantly bound copies of Juvenal and Persius and Cicero, nothing is read now but Longfellow and Hall Caine and Miss Corelli. Where good and roomy houses were built a hundred years ago, poor and tawdry houses are built now; and bad bookbinding, bad pictures, and bad decorations are thought well of, where rich bindings, beautiful miniatures and finely-carved chimney pieces were once prized by the old Irish landlords. (II. 231–1)

In both the nomad and the nobleman Synge found aristocracy of taste. His emotions, however, were complex. He admired the independence and perceptiveness of the beggar while pitying him for his times of wretchedness. He admired the cultured tastes of the eighteenth-century landlord while deploring his oppression of the peasantry. He, like Yeats, had a 'dream of the noble and the beggarman', and, like Yeats, could not really contrive a political programme that would protect those virtues bred of social situations of which he could not approve.

Synge's vision of what is most essentially Irish and national is, moreover, as much a vision of a spiritual ambience as anything else. It is a vision of simplicity which can as often lead to violence, drunkenness and ribaldry as to quiet courtesy, gentleness, and long slow conversations upon the wonders of the world and the days that are gone. It is a vision of men naked to the natural forces that surround them, who live in a country where the twilights are filled with 'vague and passionate anguish' and the sunlit glens with exuberant vitality. In the Wicklow glens the old people met on the roads will talk for hours to a wanderer:

... telling him stories of the Rebellion, or of the fallen angels that ride across the hills, or alluding to the three shadowy countries that are never forgotten in Wicklow – America (their El Dorado), the Union and the Madhouse.

(II. 216)

Though isolated and ignorant, these people are often in a way more European than their fellows in Dublin and other cities. They have tales of travellers, and their stories are part of the basic stuff of European culture. Moreover, there are dim memories of ancient wisdom. In Kerry a man tells Synge:

There is a plant ... which is the richest that is growing out of the ground, and in the old times the women used to be giving it to their children till they'd be growing up seven feet maybe in height. Then the priests and doctors began taking everything to themselves and destroyed the old knowledge, and that is a poor thing; for you know well it was the Holy Mother of God who cured her own Son with plants the like of that, and said after that no mother should be without a plant for ever to cure her child. Then she threw out the seeds of it over the whole world, so that it's growing every place from that day to this.

(II. 246)

In this story we can see, as we can see in Synge's talk of walking in West Kerry where Diarmuid had fought, that dream of a golden age long past which runs through so much Irish writing of the period. Synge's view of the past is, however, more than chauvinistic. In Kerry, watching a procession of people on their way to the chapel in Ballyferriter, he found:

This procession along the olive bogs, between the mountains and the sea, on this grey day of autumn seemed to wring me with the pang of emotion one meets everywhere in Ireland – an emotion that is partly local and patriotic and partly a share of the desolation that is mixed everywhere with the supreme beauty of the world.

[II. 240]

The magnificent and the melancholy, the exuberant and the contemplative, the reticent and the exuberant, the extroverted and the introspective: these all exist at their most intense, making harmony of their discords, in the Ireland which Synge loved. Over and over again this harmony in discord is presented to us. Looking out over the sea in Kerry he perceived 'a splendour that was almost a grief in the mind' (II. 280), and in almost all his stories the spiritual and the gross, the rude and the delicate, the earthy and the spiritual, blend together.

Though Synge was, in his essays on Wicklow and Kerry, clearly attempting to portray a life that he felt to reveal the essence of the Irish, his description does not provide him with any sociological solutions. He is contemplating a wonder, and not analysing a society. It is worth recording that when in 1909 he thought of doing more articles for the *Guardian* he suggested not another study of economic problems, but a series on 'Irish Types'. In 'Under Ether' (1897) he wrote:

I took notice of every familiar occurrence as if it were something I had come back to from a distant country . . .   (II. 43)

and it is with this wondering intensity of awareness that he wrote of Wicklow and Kerry. The 1907 revision of *Vita Vecchia* contains a paragraph I have already quoted which should perhaps be repeated here:

We do wrong to seek a foundation for ecstasy in philosophy or the hidden things of the spirit – if there is spirit – for when life is at its simplest, with nothing beyond or before it, the mystery is greater than we can endure.
(II. 24)

If Synge had a programme for Ireland, it was one of awakening it to its own spiritual richness; Home Rule could perhaps help in this awakening. Land reform and increased help for the wretched in the distressed areas could free them of material anxiety and permit them to build upon the few remaining fragments of their ancient culture. Opposed to thrusting Gaelic down the throats of all his countrymen, he felt nevertheless that the good Irish dialects of the west should not be lost, for their loss would mean also the loss of much music and poetry. Believing all these things, he was opposed to bourgeois capitalism, to the rule of the shopkeepers, and, though his mother thought him a socialist, his temperament was opposed to authoritarianism and organized government and very much sympathetic towards increasing the liberty of the individual, which included the liberty to opt out from modern Europe and the 'seedy town life most of us are condemned to'.

He was intent upon matters we may call spiritual, yet he wrote in a notebook of 1908:

The religious art is a thing of the past only – a vain and foolish regret – and its place has been taken by our quite modern feeling for the beauty and mystery [of] nature, an emotion that has gradually risen up as religion in the dogmatic sense has gradually died. Our pilgrimages are not to Canterbury or Jerusalem, but to Killarney and Cumberland and the Alps. . . . In my plays and topographical books I have tried to give humanity and this mysterious external world. (II. 351)

In the same notebook he wrote:

Man has gradually grown up in this world that is about us, and I think that while Tolstoy is wrong in claiming that art should be intelligible to the peasant, he is right in seeking a criterion for the arts, and I think this is to be found in testing art by its compatibility with the outside world and the peasants or people who live near it. A book, I mean, that one feels ashamed to read in a cottage of Dingle Bay one may fairly call a book that is not healthy – or universal. (II. 351)

Even in his most local and 'topographical' book Synge sought to express the universal. He sought to express it in terms of Ireland, and he sought to indicate how Ireland itself could develop her awareness of universal elements of the human condition by studying and sharing the life of those nomads and peasants who, in ignorant simplicity, however victimized by events, retained some shreds of the 'old knowledge' and were in harmony with the earth.

CHAPTER TEN

The Playboy of the Western World

Synge began writing *The Playboy of the Western World* in September 1904. At first he called it *The Murderer* (*A Farce*), and his rough scenario told only of the 'murder' (Act One), the 'murderer's boastings' (Act Two), and of his being elected county councillor, only to be faced at his hour of triumph with his 'resurrected' father (Act Three). In the winter of 1904–5 the plan was expanded to include the Widow Quin, Pegeen, and Shawn. Thereafter the numerous drafts show a continual process of development. The Widow Quin several times appears about to dominate the play and her part has to be readjusted to the demands of the whole. By 5 November 1906 Synge could tell Lady Gregory: 'I have only very little now to do to the Playboy to get him *provisionally* finished.' On 8 November he was of the opinion that: 'A little verbal correction is still necessary and one or two structural points may need – I fancy do need – revision.' He read Lady Gregory and Yeats the first two acts on 13 November, and the third on 28 November. On 31 December he handed over acts one and two to the Abbey, and the third act was handed over a little later. On 8 January 1907 the play went into rehearsal and many cuts were made at this time. The strong language of the play caused anxiety among the cast and the directors. On 26 January the play was performed and, as is well known, the restive audience rose in uproar at the word 'shifts' in the third act. In spite of over fifty cuts that had been made during rehearsal, it was clear that the play retained enough vitality to disturb its audience.

The history of this first 'Playboy row', and of the other rows in

America does not concern us here. The consequence of the rows, however, was that Synge himself was obliged to comment both in public and in private on his own play. In the programme note for the first production he maintained:

. . . I have used very few words that I have not heard among the country people, or spoken in my own childhood before I could read the news-papers. . . .   (IV. 363)

After the first-night riot Synge was reported as telling the *Evening Mail* that he had not attempted 'to represent Irish life as it is lived', and as saying:

I wrote the play because it pleased me, and it just happens that I know Irish life best, so I made my methods Irish.[14]

He was reported as calling his play 'a comedy, an extrava-ganza, made to amuse', and saying, 'I never bother whether my plots are typically Irish or not; but my methods are typical.'

Synge's own account of what he said in that interview is included in a letter to Stephen MacKenna:

He – the interviewer – got in my way – may the devil bung a cesspool with his skull – and said, 'Do you really think, Mr Synge, that if a man did this in Mayo, girls would bring him a pullet?' The next time it was, 'Do you think, Mr Synge, they'd bring him eggs?' I lost my poor temper (God forgive me that I didn't wring his neck) and I said, 'Oh well, if you like, it's impossible, it's extravagance (how's it spelt?). So is *Don Quixote*!' He hashed up what I said a great [deal] worse than I expected, but I wrote next day politely backing out of all that was in the interview. That's the whole myth. It isn't quite accurate to say, I think, that the thing is a generalization from a simple case. If the idea had occurred to me I could and would just as readily have written the thing as it stands without the Lynchehaun case or the Aran case. The story – in its *essence* – is probable, given the psychic state of the locality. I used the cases afterwards to controvert critics who said it was *impossible*.[15]

The Lynchehaun case and the Aran case are both instances of men being wanted by the police for murder being given sanc-tuary by the peasants. The letter to MacKenna makes it clear that Synge's claim to naturalistic reporting was, in this case as in others, a defensive response to criticism. The reference to *Don Quixote* is intriguing and worth bearing in mind.

The letter which Synge wrote to the press as a consequence of the interview is also significant. Synge explained:

'The Playboy of the Western World' is not a play with 'a purpose' in the modern sense of the word, but although parts of it are, or are meant to be, extravagant comedy, still a great deal more that is behind it, is perfectly serious when looked at in a certain light. That is often the case, I think, with comedy, and no one is quite sure to-day whether 'Shylock' and 'Alceste' should be played seriously or not. There are, it may be hinted, several sides to 'The Playboy'. 'Pat', I am glad to notice, has seen some of them in his own way. There may be still others if anyone cares to look for them.

(IV. 364)

'Pat' was Patrick Kenny, who had seen the play largely as a prophecy of the downfall of an Ireland that was exporting its strongest inhabitants and being emotionally and spiritually debilitated by the institution of arranged and loveless marriages. Another interpretation was offered by the *Evening Mail* reviewer, who thought the play might be an allegory, though he found it too obscure for him. He suggested that 'the parricide represents some kind of nation-killer, whom Irish men and Irish women hasten to lionize'. Most reviewers, however, took a more naïve line. The *Freeman's Journal* saw the play as an 'unmitigated, protracted libel upon Irish peasant men and, worse still upon Irish girlhood', and referred to it as a 'squalid, offensive production, incongruously styled a comedy ...'. D. J. O'Donoghue, in a letter to the same paper, said:

The continuous ferocity of the language, the consistent shamelessness of all the characters (without exception), and the persistent allusions to sacred things make the play even more inexcusable as an extravaganza than as a serious play. . . .[16]

In a letter to M. J. Nolan of 19 February Synge wrote:

With a great deal of what you say I am most heartily in agreement – as where you see that I wrote the P.B. directly, as a piece of life, without thinking or caring to think, whether it was a comedy tragedy or extravaganza, or whether it would be held to have, or not to have, a purpose – also where you speak very accurately and rightly about Shakespeare's 'mirror'. In the same way you see . . . that the wildness and, if you will, vices of the Irish peasantry are due, like their extraordinary good points of all kinds, to the *richness* of their nature – a thing that is priceless beyond words. . . . Whether or not I agree with your final interpretation of the whole play is my secret. I follow Goethe's rule to tell no one what one means in one's writings.

(IV. xxiii)

If we add together all these public and private comments of Synge we get a fairly clear notion, not of the precise 'meaning' he himself attached to his play, but of his attitudes towards the play's message element. Firstly, he insists that the play is credible in terms of actuality, but should not be labelled comedy, tragedy or extravaganza. He suggests that there are 'several sides' to the play, and, while calling it 'a piece of life', indicates that it does have a meaning or meanings and is more than a simple piece of entertainment. He clearly indicates the central ambiguity of mood by his reference to Shylock and Alceste, and also, more significantly, by his reference, when being questioned by a reporter, to *Don Quixote*. Don Quixote is, like Christie Mahon, a fantasist and an 'outsider'. He was used by Cervantes to comment upon the vices and absurdities of the society of his time. He is himself a fool, but ultimately much less of a fool than the acceptably conventional realists he encounters, for his folly and his fantasy are supported and dignified by a view of the world which is obsessively idealistic and chivalrous, whereas the other people lack any real conviction or vision. Moreover, in several instances, Quixote persuades others to share for a while his fantasy and to see themselves as fair ladies, nobles and knights, in a world of dragons and heroism. Sometimes self-consciously, sometimes humorously or even derisively, they gain through him a sense of the glories that are gone and of the dignity they no longer feel they possess. Finally, however, Quixote is most usually rejected, and rides away, accompanied by his faithful, awed, yet sceptical Sancho Panza, to find new wonders and irradiate other commonplaces with the ideal illumination of his fantasy.

It is not difficult to see Christy Mahon as a Don Quixote figure, at once saviour and fool, hero and clown, visionary and madman. The difference is that it is, at least in part, the peasants who create the vision for him. Initially he is only a scared boy, convinced in his simplicity that he has killed his father. Praised and admired for his derring-do, he becomes both a braggart and a visionary, his words elevating the commonplace into such poetry that Pegeen Mike and even the Widow Quin are dazzled by his eloquence. Inspired thus he becomes, in fact, the hero, winning all the prizes at the races, and though finally he falls from grace when his father returns from the dead, he retains at the close of the action that heroic self-confidence which he has been given.

It is at the end of the play, however, that the Quixote element gives way to another, for Christy again 'kills' his father and is immediately viewed with horror and both beaten and betrayed.

It is here that Synge's Shylock parallelism applies. As long as Shylock's 'bargain' remained a distant threat and a fantasy Bassanio regarded him amiably. When, however, he attempted to perform in reality what had been disregarded when merely imagined, he was not only regarded with horror but condemned for a crime of conspiracy which had previously been tolerated and even jested over. The parallelism is obviously inexact, but points to Synge's understanding the essential part played by that element of the grotesque and brutal which some of his audience condemned. In one of his sketches for the play Synge, as in *The Tinker's Wedding* plan, attached descriptive epithets to each movement and each small episode. The first act he saw as moving from 'comedy and locality' through 'Molièrian climax of farce', 'savoury dialogue', 'Poetical', 'Rabelaisian' to the final 'diminuendo ironical'. The second act uses the words 'character', 'comedy' and 'Poetical' to describe its shape. In the third act alone, after Old Mahon and Christy meet face to face, is the word 'drama' used (IV. 296–7). At that point, indeed, the whole play alters its perspective and characters once found endearing are found to be ignorant, vicious and treacherous.

George Moore recognized this shift in the play when he wanted Synge to alter the ending, saying, 'Your end is not comedy, it ends on a disagreeable note.' Moore found the physical violence at the end most unacceptable.

The burning of Christy's legs with the coal is quite intolerable and wouldn't be acceptable to any audience – French, German or Russian. The audience doesn't mind what is said, but what is done – the father coming in with his head bandaged with a dangerous make-up.[17]

Moore later recanted, but his letter must have entertained Synge, for surely one of the points made about the Mayo folk is that they don't 'mind what is said, but what is done', a point which could only be driven home by the emphasis upon physical actuality provided by the coal incident and the bloody head of Old Mahon actually 'killed' in front of them.

It is at this point that the relationship between language and actuality comes into the picture. Throughout the play there has been, to quote D. J. O'Donoghue, 'continuous ferocity of language'. The action itself, however, only erupts into violence the once, and, as Pegeen Mike says, 'there's a great gap between a gallous story and a dirty deed' (IV. 169). It is not only the ferocity of the language that is important; it is what O'Donoghue calls 'the persistent allusions to sacred things'.

That the play constantly uses religious words is obvious enough. The first impression one receives is that the almost indiscriminate appeals to divinity are intended to point to the use of Christian terminology as a medium for imprecation and a vehicle for superstition. The dignity of the references contrasts with the pettiness of their occasion. It is one way to create comic incongruity and show the spiritual decadence of the west, a decadence which has gone so far that, for all the religious verbiage, the only acceptable Redeemer turns out to be a young man who has killed his Da in a scuffle, not Christ Messiah but Christy Mahon.

Once the notion of Christy as in some way related to Christ enters the picture, however, it is likely to dominate it. Stanley Sultan, in a well argued essay,[18] presents a view of Christy as a Promethean figure whose rebellion against his father symbolizes for the Mayo peasants their wish to revolt against the oppressive forces of the Church as represented by 'the Holy Father' in Rome and 'Father Reilly' nearer at hand. 'Stop tormenting me with Father Reilly,' cries Pegeen to Shawn, she being the girl most attracted to the heroic view of parricide. Dr Sultan, however, goes on from this to suggest that 'the *Playboy* presents a carefully developed analogue to the ministry and crucifixion of Jesus'.

At first blush this may seem an extreme view, but once the analogy has been hypothesized a number of details appear to support it. The village girls bring the newly arrived Christy 'presents' and announce 'Well, you're a marvel! Oh, God bless you! You're the lad surely!' (IV. 103), thus parodying the Epiphany. The triumphant entry of Christy into the house after his ride to victory in the sports, applauded by all the crowds, is followed, after a while, by a judgment scene in which the crowd's mood changes. The episode begins when the betrothal of Pegeen and Christy is blessed by Michael:

... so may God and Mary and St Patrick bless you, and increase you from this mortal day.
CHRISTY *and* PEGEEN: Amen, O Lord! (IV. 157)

Old Mahon then rushes in and identifies himself. Pegeen is convinced and turns on Christy:

CHRISTY: You've seen my doings this day, and let you save me from the old man; for why would you be in such a scorch of haste to spur me to destruction now?
PEGEEN: It's there your treachery is spurring me, till I'm hard set to think you're the one I'm after lacing in my heart strings half-an-hour gone by. *To* MAHON. Take him on from this, for I think bad the world should see me raging for a Munster liar and the fool of men.
MAHON: Rise up now to retribution, and come on with me.
CROWD *jeeringly*: There's the playboy! There's the lad thought he'd rule the roost in Mayo. Slate him now, Mister.
CHRISTY *getting up in shy terror*: What is it drives you to torment me here, when I'd ask the thunders of the might of God to blast me if I ever did hurt to any saving only that one single blow.
MAHON *loudly*: If you didn't, you're a poor good-for-nothing, and isn't it by the like of you the sins of the whole world are committed?
CHRISTY *raising his hands*: In the name of the Almighty God. . . . (IV. 161–2)

The echoes of the New Testament here are indisputable. In other parts of the play we are reminded of the parable of the Good Samaritan, when the moaning stranger is left to himself 'in the gripe of the ditch' by Shawn and Michael. The binding and wounding of Christy echoes the binding and wounding of Christ and his projected hanging recalls the crucifixion. Pegeen's betrayal of him is Judas-like; after offering intense affection she brings him total betrayal. If we see Christy Mahon as a distorted reflection of Christ Messiah, then we can see Father Reilly and the Holy Father and Shawn Keogh as representatives of the Old Testament religion and those Saducees and Pharisees whom Christ opposed. That the hypothesis we posited has some basis is clear enough. Dr Sultan, however, is more emphatic than we might wish. He says:

. . . what Synge has concretely presented is a mirror-image of the story of Jesus' mission of exhortation to obedience to His Father. And it is this fact which makes the sudden and shocking reversal in the last minutes of the play comprehensible. Like Jesus, when Christy confronts with the true significance of his message those who have followed and praised him, they prepare to have him executed by the standard method used for common criminals. The crucifixion is no less complete and sudden a reversal in a triumphant short earthly career; and it came about precisely because the people would not risk secular and spiritual trouble when the issue arose.

Later in his essay he says:

It is through his exploitation in *Playboy* of the ministry and crucifixion of Jesus that Synge crystallized the elements of the play into a coherent master-piece. The analogue both helps to motivate, and articulates precisely the nature of the reciprocal effects of Christy on the people of Mayo and the people on him. Furthermore, the comic action of Christy's glorification and reunion with his father, and the bitter denouement of rejection and betrayal, are not disparate but integral: the Christ analogue simply and eloquently establishes that they are complementary to each other in a single pattern.

The trouble with this view of the *Playboy* is that the Christ analogue is intermittent. We cannot easily avoid believing in the Christy-Christ parallelism at the judgment scene; apart from anything else Old Mahon's rhetorical question, 'Isn't it by the like of you the sins of the whole world are committed?' (IV. 161), reminds one instantaneously of that Christ who took upon him all the sins of the world. The parallelism with the Good Samaritan story is also extremely obvious. Nevertheless, we would have to be ludicrously ingenious to find similarly exact counterparts to the love-talk between Christy and Pegeen (should we see her as the Church, the bride of Christ?), to Widow Quinn (the temptation in the wilderness?) and the double 'death' of Old Mahon (the Nativity and the Resurrection?). It would be better, perhaps, to consider one or two more fundamental attributes of the play before allowing ingenuity to outdistance reason.

The Playboy of the Western World is, in my definition, a shan-achie play. It originated, at least partly, in a story told Synge by Pat Dirane, the shanachie of Inishmaan. If we look at the other stories told Synge by shanachies, especially in the Aran islands, we may be able to get another perspective upon the play.

The first thing that strikes one about the stories, as opposed to the anecdotes, that Synge heard, is their extraordinary richness of echo. Synge himself pointed to this when he related the story of O'Connor to *Cymbeline*, to the *Two Merchants and the Faithful Wife of Ruprecht von Würzburg*, and to the *Gesta Romanorum*. Other stories have the same characteristic. A story of Diarmuid parallels that of the Shirt of Nessus. Another long story, that of the widow's son who, having killed a great many flies, thinks himself a hero and goes out into the world, has echoes of several of Grimm's stories, Greek myths, and medieval romances. Indeed, all the stories told Synge on Aran and elsewhere could be analysed as conflations of several older stories, and most of them contain archetypal elements.

If we look at the structure of the *Playboy* in these terms it becomes apparent that it has several characteristics in common both with the shanachie story and the shanachie anecdote. Firstly the material of the play has been created from many disparate sources. Dr Saddlemyer lists three passages from *The Aran Islands*, twelve from *In Wicklow, West Kerry and Connemara*, and five from various notebooks (IV. 360–2), and all these, either in language or theme, relate directly to different parts of the play. Moreover, the 'Good Samaritan' episode in the *Playboy* relates to the death of Patch Darcy in *The Shadow of the Glen*; Christy telling us he is 'handy with ewes' is reminiscent of the use of that image in the same play, and the 'poet's talking' of Christy recalls the 'poetry' of the Douls in *The Well of the Saints*. Christy says to Pegeen:

Let you wait to hear me talking till we're astray in Erris when Good Friday's by, drinking a sup from a well, and making mighty kisses with our wetted mouths, or gaming in a gap of sunshine with yourself stretched back unto your necklace in the flowers of the earth. (IV. 149)

Martin Doul says to Molly Byrne:

Let you come on now, I'm saying, to the lands of Ivereagh and the Reeks of Cork, where you won't set down the width of your two feet and not be crushing fine flowers, and making sweet smells in the air. (IV. 117)

Some of these echoes of earlier writings may have been un-conscious, but Synge's own defensive emphasis upon his play's actuality makes it clear that he was aware of the conglomerate character of his work. Moreover, as one looks through the worksheets for the *Playboy* there are numerous indications of a highly conscious process of gathering, reconstructing, and paring.

If, then, the *Playboy* is as conglomerate as many of the shanachie tales in its fusing together of separate events and ascribing them all to one occasion, does it have other attributes of those tales also?

It is here that the mythic element in the *Playboy* falls into place. Just as the O'Connor story can be related, at different places, to several older and archetypal stories and legends, so *The Playboy of the Western World* can, at different times, be related with differing degrees of precision to the New Testa-ment, to *Don Quixote*, and to stories current among the folk of the west of Ireland. Synge has, indeed, not only created a play from shanachie material; he has created a play which has precisely the same kind of richness as the shanachie material, a play fitfully illuminated by archetypal echoes and allusions, which, nevertheless, retains coherence, not upon the mythic, but upon the narrative level. The 'psychic state of the locality' is expressed in a language of such strength that it dominates and unifies the play. *The Playboy of the Western World* is not allegory or parable or myth or anti-myth. If it must be given a label, the label must be invented, for the method of con-struction and the manipulation of echo and theme are entirely original, and very few other playwrights have profited by Synge's discoveries. Among these, however, and obviously, is Sean O'Casey whose mature drama uses the same shifting levels of meaning, the same intermittent symbolist power, and the same ferocity and lyricism of speech.

This view of the *Playboy* relates it closely to Synge's other work, and permits us to see that the basic technique of con-glomeration alters little from *When the Moon Has Set* and *The Aran Islands* to the later work. Nevertheless, just as *The Aran Islands* is, in its symphonic construction of impressions, more than a simple retelling of collected experiences, so the *Playboy*, while being typical of shanachie tales in its manipulation of anecdote and archetype, is much more than an extravaganza. While the plot is simple, the language is not, and the characters act as vehicles for themes of which they themselves are unaware. This is typical of Synge. One cannot suppose that Maurya knew of Hippolitus or Nora Casey of the Widow of Ephesus, any more than one can believe that Martin Doul saw his rebellion against the saint in other than terms of purely private necessity. In all Synge's drama, after *When the Moon Has Set*, where the themes are consciously presented by the hero, the characters embody or exemplify attitudes and principles of universal significance. They are thus, every one of them, to a greater or lesser extent, ironic creations, for they are unaware of their own cosmic significance as exemplars and embodiments, while struggling desperately to achieve lesser dignities. *Deirdre of the Sorrows* is the only exception to this rule. There is pathos in this, as when Martin Doul prefers his physical blindness to the spiritual blindness of the saint and unwittingly epitomizes heroically one aspect of the Protestant ethic and the principle of dissent, and as when Sarah Casey, the embodiment of all culturally rich yet deprived minorities, seeks a respectability less filled with dignity than the individualism of her own tradition.

In the *Playboy*, however, the central character arrives, though confusedly, at an understanding of his own symbolic standing, and thus, at the close of the play, triumphs not only over his rejection by the society that first admired him, but also over the irony which is inherent in all human yearnings after dignity. He is, in some ways, the counterpart to Luasnad who, recognizing the manipulation of the gods, yet, in a moment of tragedy, asserts the presence of individual passion and will. Christy Mahon, displaced, rejected, and bereaved of the object of his love, does not, like Maurya, keen at the mortal lot, like Nora express fear of the freedom rebellion has at last brought, or like Sarah Casey return, with only a modicum of increased awareness, to the life she has previously wished to alter; nor does he, like Martin Doul, face the consequences of his rebellion with a stoic dignity and a dream of romance: he exults in his understanding of his own dionysiac potential, and walks away from Mayo with a Yea and not a Nay upon his lips.

That Synge, in working out his play, thought in terms of character as much as theme is clearly observable from the work-sheets. There are continual changes in speeches, but almost all appear to be made in order to clarify the relationships of the characters and make the development of the plot more credible. There are no crudely symbolist speeches, as there are in the drafts of *The Tinker's Wedding*. Queries and hesitations relate to human encounters rather than to archetypal references, though it is noticeable that in the discarded drafts there are many uses of religious terminology and these increase as the play proceeds. It was, it appears, from a rigorous exploration of 'the psychic state of the locality' and of the inter-relationship of characters, each a vehicle for attitudes and principles endemic in that locality, that Synge developed the mythic richness which Stanley Sultan sees as a Christian analogue that coheres and dignifies the drama.

If this is the case it might be as well to consider the characters of the play and their functions. It would be interesting, indeed, to do this in depth, and to study the way in which each character developed throughout the numerous drafts. This would, however, be a book in itself, and in the present book I am concerned with Synge's creative procedures only in as far as they illuminate the finished work, and with his discarded materials only in so far as they point to aspects of the plays which might otherwise escape detection or be merely suspected and not proven.

It seems reasonable to dispose of some minor characters fairly summarily. Philly O'Cullen and Jimmy Farrell are, like the voices of the crowd, largely used to express collective feeling. Their first major part is played in the cross-examining of Christy where they show something of the 'psychic state of the locality'. Jimmy establishes Christy's masculinity by thinking he may be being hunted for following 'a young woman on a lonesome night' (IV. 69). Philly reveals the general attitude to landowners by suggesting that 'maybe the land was grabbed from him and he did what any decent man would do' (IV. 69). Philly says: 'Well that lad's a puzzle-the-world,' and Jimmy agrees: 'He'd beat Dan Davies' Circus or the holy missioners making sermons on the villainy of man' (IV. 71).

Thus Jimmy reveals that the moral content of religion is of less importance to him than its value as entertainment, and that he finds the diatribes of the missionaries as delightfully inexplicable as the feats of the circus performers. Philly gives us crude nationalism in his suggestion that Christy may be one of those who had fought on the Boer side in the war and who were now liable to be 'judged to be hanged, quartered and drawn' (IV. 71). (An earlier draft of this speech [IV. 70] made a more explicit reference to 'Major MacBride, God shield him, who's afear'd to put the tip of his nose into Ireland fearing he'd be hanged quartered and drawn'.) Both Philly and Jimmy are convinced that Pegeen would be safe with a man like Christy in the house, and that the 'peelers' would be afraid of him, and thus indicate the general view of legality as an irrelevance.

In the second act the two men are not present. Their picture of the situation is here enlarged and modified by the four girls Nelly, Sara, Susan and Honor. (In the first production there were only three girls, Nelly's speeches being given to Honor.) They bring Christy gifts, thus parodying the Epiphany. Sara reveals the kind of heroes they approve of when she says to both Widow Quin (who is reputed to have killed her husband) and Christy:

You're heroes surely, and let you drink a supeen with your arms linked like the outlandish lovers in the sailor's song. There now. Drink a health to the wonders of the western world, the pirates, preachers, poteen-makers, with the jobbing jockies, parching peelers, and the juries fill their stomachs selling judgments of the English law. (IV. 105)

The lumping together of the preachers with the pirates and poteen-makers, and of the peelers with the jockies and bribed juries, indicates the cynical realism as well as the romantic love of wildness and roguery which is characteristic of this western world.

In Act Three, Jimmy and Philly act at first as chorus and then as commentators upon the sports on the strand, and bring a touch of the grotesque into the play by their talk of bones and skulls. Philly says:

. . . when I was a young lad, there was a graveyard beyond the house with the remnants of a man who had thighs as long as your arm. He was a horrid man, I'm telling you, and there was many a fine Sunday I'd put him together for fun, and he with shiny bones you wouldn't meet the like of these days in the cities of the world.

Mahon replies:

You wouldn't is it? Lay your eyes on that skull, and tell me where there was another the like of it, is splintered only from the blow of a loy.   (IV. 135)

Philly's reference may be to one of the ancient Irish heroes. Finn's reputed grave just off the Westport–Murrisk road is on a hill above a farm and is twenty feet long. It may be of this Synge is thinking or of other stories of the stature of the warriors of the past. The result in the play, however, is to establish Christy's deed as comparable to those of the Fianna. Later in this act, Philly and Jimmy and their fellows take part in the binding of Christy after Old Mahon has been 'killed' a second time.

Thus Philly and Jimmy and the four girls play chorus and initially help to build up the picture of the mores of the society in which Christy finds himself. Michael's role in the play is scarcely more substantial. He serves to emphasize the cowardice of Shawn Keogh, to underline the bibulous aspect of the society, to parody religious ceremonial in his blessing of Pegeen and Christy, and to lead in the binding of Christy in the third act. It is he, however, who decides that it is better to breed 'little gallant swearers' by Christy than 'puny weeds' by Shawn Keogh, for all Shawn's wealth (IV. 157).

Shawn Keogh is of most importance at the beginning of the play where he displays his cowardice and his total subservience to the will of the Church. He has no will of his own, wondering if he would have the 'right' to visit Pegeen, expressing fear of the dark, showing his selfishness in his running away from the groaning man in the ditch, and telling all that he is 'afeard of Father Reilly'. Though godfearing he is also treacherous. When Widow Quinn tells him:

It's true all girls are fond of courage and do hate the like of you . . .

he replies:

Oh, Widow Quin, what'll I be doing now? I'd inform again him, but he'd burst from Kilmainham and he'd be sure and certain to destroy me. If I wasn't so Godfearing, I'd near have courage to come behind him and run a pike into his side.   (IV. 117)

In his attempting to bribe Widow Quin to marry Christy, and in his telling Michael James that if Christy marries Pegeen he will lose the promised 'drift of heifers' and the 'blue bull from Sneem' (IV. 155), he exposes the materialism of the peasants.

It is with Pegeen Mike, the Widow Quin and Christy Mahon that we should be most concerned. Pegeen Mike differs from the other girls in the energy of her passions, the liveliness of her tongue, and the decisiveness of her temper. Rejecting Shawn Keogh, she also rejects the paternal authoritarianism of the Church, as she, too, pays little heed to the authority of her own father. Attracted by Christy, she uses him to further her search for identity, freedom, and romance, finding his words and his deeds heroic and poetic. When Old Mahon returns to life she is angered by having been fooled. When Old Mahon is killed the second time and Christy set upon and tied, it is she who leads in the tying and it is she who ruthlessly burns him with the lighted turf. Pegeen's intensity of feeling leads her towards both total acceptance and total rejection. Her spirit is akin to the Playboy's in its extreme vitality, and it is this that attracts her to him and also causes her to reject him.

Pegeen contrasts with Widow Quin who, like the village girls, finds Christy attractive, but, unlike Pegeen, does not expect integrity in her hero. She is not too perturbed by the arrival of Old Mahon, and delightedly connives at the suppression of the true facts. She herself wants Christy as her man, but her morality is dubious. She offers him other girls as if she were to be his procuress rather than his bride, and her view of life appears to be totally unprincipled. She is a strong character in the play and dominates most of the action when she is on stage. By her candid self-seeking she reveals the moral confusion of her friends and neighbours. They swear by their God, and take His name in vain. The Widow rarely uses the name of God. Indeed, in the whole play she uses the word only twice. The first occasion is when she tells Christy:

When you see me contriving in my little gardens, Christy Mahon, you'll swear the Lord God formed me to be living lone and that there isn't my match in Mayo for thatching or mowing or shearing a sheep.   (IV. 89)

The second is when she says of Pegeen to Christy:

God help her to be taking you for a wonder, and you a little schemer making up a story you destroyed your da.   (IV. 125)

Her attitude to the hectic religious language of the others is well shown when Christy asks her to help him win Pegeen.

CHRISTY: . . . Aid me for to win her, and I'll be asking God to stretch a hand to you in the hour of death, and lead you short cuts through the Meadows of Ease, and up the floor of Heaven to the Footstool of the Virgin's Son.
WIDOW QUIN: There's praying!   (IV. 129–31)

The Widow Quin observes the goings-on with a mixture of detached amusement, sympathy, and mischievous opportunism. She sees Christy and Pegeen for what they are.

This, however, is her limitation. For Christy's world is not the real one. It is a world of high words and great claims, and he is so intoxicated and elevated by his dream that he actually makes it come true. He does show himself a leader of men, in that he wins the contests on the sands, as if he were a hero at the Greek games. He is admired by the girls and, even after his downfall, he retains some of their affection. Moreover, while he does not become a father-killer, he does become his father's master. Words have created the reality they pictured. Moreover, he now understands the importance of having a proper conceit of himself, and knowing his dignity as a unique human creature. This has been given him as much by the times of glory as by the hours of defeat. For all his blusterings, his elaborate appeals to the heavenly powers, and his confusions of Christian values, he has discovered something which is more important than Pegeen's belief in the need for integrity, and than Widow Quin's materialist realism, and than Shawn Keogh's submission to his Church. He embodies the wildness, the richness, the idealism and the romanticism of the west in his own person, and he has found that it is possible to transfigure existence with the poetry of energy and passion.

Rejecting Christy, Pegeen realizes that she has rejected the only one who had the secret of transforming the dullness of life into radiance. She herself made him; she, with her passion for idealism and rebellion, convinced him of his own glory, but then the creation outdistanced the creator who became afraid of the creature she had invented. Pegeen is, after all, no more than a village girl and, at least according to the Widow Quin, not particularly exceptional. Christy, however, is exceptional. He becomes much more than a village hero. He becomes an orphic figure whose music survives his destruction. He becomes, indeed, an immortal, for he sees himself living out a 'romping lifetime from this hour to the dawning of the judgment day' (IV. 173).

Pegeen is another of Synge's passionate, disturbed women hungry for freedom and romance, and she comes closer to success than her predecessors. Nevertheless, her pride and the fundamental puritanism of her temperament make it impossible for her to accept the consequences of her own dream. She cannot accept the Romancer that is Christy, nor can she face his loss without grief. She represents an Ireland that dreaming of independence cannot accept the consequences of the dream becoming reality any more than that faith in spiritual power to which she gives lip service. For Christy is a representative of faith and spiritual power. He will be 'master of all fights from now' (IV. 173), because of that faith. Poverty of spirit is the disease Pegeen and all Ireland must recognize.

It is now that the utility of the Christ-Christy analogue can be seen. Christy is a poor man who achieves spiritual authority by pursuing, through times of weakness and despair, a vision of freedom that transfigures his own life and that of the people about him. His betrayal and crucifixion cannot break his spirit. He faces death and hell with courage and gaiety. Betrayed by those who crowned him king, he nevertheless triumphs. A parody of Christ rather than a reflection of Him, he gives the society he enters the exact leader they wish for – one of those whom Pegeen describes when she laments the passing of the great ones of the past such as 'Daneen Sullivan knocked the eye from a peeler' and Marcus Quin who told 'stories of holy Ireland till he'd have the old women shedding down tears about their feet' (IV. 59). Societies get the leaders they deserve and Christy Mahon is more fitted for Mayo than Christ Messiah, but even Christy is betrayed. There is no wonder perhaps that this play aroused many of its more perceptive but over-sensitive spectators to fury.

CHAPTER ELEVEN

Deirdre of the Sorrows

Synge appears to have been first attracted to the story of Deirdre in 1900 or 1901 when he made a rough translation of the version of *The Fate of the Children of Uisneach* published by the Society for the Preservation of the Irish Language in 1898. The story is of the eighth or ninth century, and has been variously called, in English, *The Exile of the Sons of Uisliu*, or *Uisnech*, or *Usna*. Synge wrote to Molly Allgood in December 1906: 'My next play must be quite different from the P.Boy. I want to do something quiet and stately and restrained and I want you to act in it' (IV. xxvii).

Almost two years later his letters are full of his struggles with the play. He first made notes for it in 1907, and he completed a draft in three acts on 1 December 1908, reporting that 'yesterday' he had finished 'the 8th revision or rewriting of Act III'. He was not, however, satisfied, and continued to rewrite and revise. He was still working on it in January 1909, and he left behind him a manuscript labelled 'Unfinish[ed] play of "Deirdre", can be sent if desired to Mr W. B. Yeats' (IV. xxvii–xxix). The play as published by the Cuala Press in 1910, and as played at the Abbey Theatre on 13 January 1910 under the direction of Maire O'Neill (Molly Allgood), is a draft made up of several typescripts of different dates, though each version of each act is the latest one Synge achieved. Nevertheless, in their work on this material, Yeats, Lady Gregory, and Molly Allgood did not succeed in incorporating all Synge's alterations, and were apparently unaware of some notebook material. Dr Saddlemyer's version of the play in the Oxford edition takes into account all the relevant material and is, therefore, the only acceptable text.

Having said this, it must nevertheless also be said that while there are very many differences of detail between the Cuala and the Oxford texts, the overall mood and structure of the play remains the same, and the variations do little to alter the characters and the development of the story, which is as simple as is usual with Synge. Pared of all detail, and ignoring those aspects which vary from version to version, it can be summarized thus:

At Deirdre's birth it was prophesied that she would, because of her beauty, bring trouble upon Ireland. Because of her the sons of Usna and Fergus would be exiled and many men killed. Conchubor, High King of Ulster, refused to have the child killed, but had her looked after until she would be old enough to be his queen. Naisi, the elder of the three sons of Usna, fell in love with her and took her into exile with him. After seven years they were persuaded to return, but Conchubor killed Naisi and his brothers and claimed Deirdre, who committed suicide.

There are so many versions of the exact nature of Deirdre's suicide, of the precise manner in which the Sons of Usna were betrayed, and of the main reasons for the return of the company to Ulster from Alban that Synge had a fairly free hand with his plot. It is, however, worth noticing what he chose to leave out. He omitted any reference to the King of Alban desiring Deirdre and thus sending her companions into dangerous situations, and he chose not to utilize the version in which Deirdre does indeed become Conchubor's mistress for a year before he gives her to another man and, in obedience to her oath never to belong to two living men, kills herself. Whereas in his earlier plays he chose rather to emphasize the violent, the brutal, and the sexual, in *Deirdre of the Sorrows* he took the opposite tack. He was, as he wrote to Molly Allgood, aiming at 'something quiet and stately and restrained'.

It is the language of *Deirdre of the Sorrows* which is particularly interesting. There are few, very few speeches in which the word-order and syntactical construction are English, and yet the vocabulary of the play is not that of colloquial Irish. Synge seems to have sought a dialect which could be pervasively Irish in its structure and yet sophisticated enough to handle that high seriousness which necessarily outlaws the vividly gross and the harshly direct. Moreover, it should be a language which could permit different levels of speech, including the simple directness of the peasant as well as the more elaborate poeticism of the high-born. It should also be, in all essentials, *poetic*.

This last conclusion may seem to be somewhat arbitrary as well as vague. It was clearly, however, a part of Synge's intention. For one thing, on 12 December 1907, when he had in fact begun work on *Deirdre*, he wrote to Frederick J. Gregg: 'I am half inclined to try a play on "Deirdre" – it would be amusing to compare it with Yeats' and Russell's . . .' (IV. xxvii). Both Yeats' and Russell's plays were, of course, in verse. In 1907 and 1908 while working on *Deirdre* he translated into prose a number of poems by Villon, Leopardi, Muset, Walter von der Vogelwiede, and Petrarch. It seems clear that, in turning these poems into an English structured in the Irish manner, he was trying to solve the problem of presenting poetry in native idiom—something which he had tried earlier in his verse drama. Moreover, he thought well enough of these experiments to include some of them in his *Poems and Translations* (1909).

Synge felt that prose was suitable for certain kinds of poetry. He tested his idea on a poem by Colin Muset which he translated both into prose and verse, and which he published in its prose version. This begins:

I'm getting old in your big house, and you've never stretched your hand with a bit of gold to me, or a day's wages itself. By my faith in Mary, it's not that way I'll serve you always, living on my pocket, with a few coppers only, and a small weight in my bag. You've had me to this day, singing on your stairs before you, but I'm getting a good mind to be going off, when I see my purse flattened out and my wife does be making a fool of me from the edge of the door. . . .   (I. 82)

The rhymed version opens:

> I'm growing old with singing on your stairs,
> And I more starving than your dogs or mares,
> Yet, by my faith in Mary, I'll not stay,
> I'll go to better men, or get my pay.

> There's gallous times when I go home at eight,
> And there's my wife to curse me at the gate. . . .   (I. 83)

Neither of these two passages is very impressive, but the two together make an important point. The words 'does be making a fool of me from the edge of the door' are extremely rhythmical but not metrical. The verse is metrical but lacks the vitality of the rhythmic prose. The mingled rhythms of the prose, its shifting speeds and surprising tricks of contrast and balance, make for a speech which can include dramatic alterations of tone and emotion more easily than the verse which Synge himself (apparently) thought appropriate at this time to dramatic soliloquy. The speech that Synge constructed for his translations is very similar to that of *Deirdre of the Sorrows*. In both cases the speech tunes are varied but all rely heavily upon balancing the number of stressed syllables in clauses and phrases. Indeed it is possible to write out many speeches as if they were in stress verse, the majority of the 'lines' having the same number of stresses, and a minority varying the tune.

> I If the birds are máking lámentátion,
>   or the gréen bánks arc móved
>   by a líttle wind of súmmer,
>   or you can heár the wáters máking a stír
>   by the shóres that are gréen and flówery   (I. 89)

> II And I'm wéll pleásed, Naísi,
>   we're góing fórward in the wínter
>   the tíme the sún has a lów pláce
>   and the móon has her mástery in a dárk ský
>   for it's yóu and Í are wéll lódged
>   our lást dáy
>   where there is a light behínd the cleár treés
>   and the bérries on the thórns are a réd wáll.   (IV. 231)

The first passage is from a translation of Petrarch and the second from *Deirdre of the Sorrows*. Both are based upon a four-stress speech unit, though both also use secondary stresses to vary and enrich the speech tune.

Both the translations and *Deirdre of the Sorrows* use a great deal of verbal and syntactical parallelism. Consider the Petrarch translation, 'He is jealous of the Heavens and the Earth'. Again, I write it out as stress verse to emphasize the structure:

> What a grudge I am bearing the earth
> that has its arms about her,
> and is holding that face away from me,
> where I was finding peace from great sadness.
>
> What a grudge I am bearing the Heavens
> that are after taking her,
> and shutting her in with greediness,
> the Heavens that do push their bolt against so many.
>
> What a grudge I am bearing the blessed saints
> that have got her sweet company,
> that I am always seeking;
>
> and what a grudge I am bearing against death
> that is standing in her two eyes
> and will not call me with a word.   (I. 91)

Here each line is a distinct clause or phrase. There are fourteen of them. Synge has in this prose version of a sonnet produced a form as highly disciplined as that of his original. If we turn now to the following passage from *Deirdre* we can see an equal discipline and a similar use of parallelism. Again I transcribe the passage as stress verse.

> There's no place to stay always. . . .
> It's a long time we've had,
> pressing the lips together,
> going up and down,
> resting in our arms, Naisi,
> waking with the smell of June
>   in the tops of the grasses,
> and listening to the birds in the branches
>   that are highest. . . .
> It's a long time we've had,
> but the end has come surely.   (IV. 231)

One could easily continue to show that *Deirdre of the Sorrows* approximates to verse in its highly disciplined use of parallelism and stress patterns by taking other passages, but perhaps the above illustrations are sufficient to make the point that in this play Synge solves one problem of poetic drama which he could not solve, at least to his own satisfaction, in the *Vernal Play*, *Luasnad, Capa and Laine*, and *Lady O'Connor*. Before going any further, however, it is worth pointing out that, though the rhythmic nature of the speech in *Deirdre* is more obvious than that of some other plays, a great deal of Synge's dramatic speech approximates to verse. Consider, for example, the following passage from *Riders to the Sea* in which the 'line' is basically one of three stresses, varied by lines of greater length:

3	They're all gone now,
5	and there isn't anything more the sea can do to me. . . .
3	I'll have no call now
3	to be up crying and praying
3	when the wind breaks from the south,
3	and you can hear the surf is in the east,
2	and the surf is in the west,
5	making a great stir with the two noises,
3	and they hitting one on the other. (III. 23–5)

From *The Shadow of the Glen*:

5	Come along with me now, lady of the house,
5	and it's not my blather you'll be hearing only,
6	but you'll be hearing the herons crying out over the black lakes,
4	and you'll be hearing the grouse and the owls with them,
5	and the larks and the big thrushes when the days are warm . . .
	(III. 57)

Similar instances can easily be found in *The Well of the Saints*, *The Tinker's Wedding*, and *The Playboy of the Western World*, though it is only in *Deirdre of the Sorrows*, of all Synge's plays, that the majority of the speeches are wrought in this rhythmic manner, and contrived of musically cadenced sentences in which the balance of clause and phrase is given harmony by the consistent use of the highly mannered locutions of Irish speech.

Unfortunately, though Synge's creation of a new medium for poetic drama may be one of his most impressive technical achievements, it is partly responsible for the comparative failure of the play as drama. The combination, in the earlier plays, of mannered and rhythmical speech with colloquial directness and even brutal coarseness not only gave those plays an interesting texture but also enriched their themes of the clash between the old and the new, the coarse and the elegant, the traditional and the contemporary. In *Deirdre of the Sorrows* Lavarcham's speeches have a trace of this tension between manner and content; Owen, whom Synge put in to give additional strength to the play, also seems intended to provide something of the same quality.

The speeches of Lavarcham and Owen, however, fall short of the vitality we might expect. Consider the following speech where Lavarcham is reported as 'jumping up with extreme annoyance':

Who says it's Conchubor's? How dare young fools the like of you (*speaking with vehement insolence*) come prying around, running the world into troubles for some slip of a girl? What brings you this place straying from Emain? *Very bitterly.* Though you think maybe young men can do their fill of foolery and there is none to blame them.   (IV. 205–7)

Such words and phrases as 'prying', 'straying', 'slip of a girl', and 'fill of foolery' are weak beside those we could reasonably expect of an angry old woman in any other play of Synge's. Consider also Owen, speaking, we are told, 'with a burst of rage'.

It's Naisi, Naisi is it? Then I'll tell you you'll have great sport one day seeing Naisi getting a harshness in his two sheep's eyes and he looking on yourself. Would you credit it, my father used to be in the broom and heather kissing Lavarcham, with a little bird chirping out above their heads, and now she'd scare a raven from a carcass on a hill. *With a sad cry that brings dignity into his voice.* Queens get old Deirdre, with their white and long arms going from them, and their backs hooping. I tell you it's a poor thing to see a queen's nose reaching down to scrape her chin.   (IV. 223)

Synge seems to have been dissatisfied with this speech, for there are question marks in the margin of his typescript. One can understand his dissatisfaction. The language lacks the rage and dignity the stage directions suggest. The element of the grotesque is not strong enough to provide dramatic shock, and the words 'would you credit it' have an air of the drawing-room wholly inappropriate to the barbarous Owen.

Restraint and stateliness did not come easily to Synge as a writer. In attempting these qualities he excluded much from his play that might have increased both its vitality and tension. He himself recognized this problem, and in writing to Molly Allgood on 6 January 1908 he said of some projected revisions: 'That – when it is done – will make the whole thing drama instead of narrative' (IV. xxviii).

Unfortunately the play remains narrative rather than drama for much of its length. This is partly because Synge chose to play down those elements of the supernatural and the ominous which he handled so effectively in *Riders to the Sea*, and which gives Yeats' *Deirdre* so much of its intensity. The sparse symbolism derives easily and naturally from the circumstances of the story, and thus does not challenge us with that sense of a powerful and alien fate manipulating the destiny of the characters which is so strong in *Luasnad, Capa and Laine*. Moreover, although Deirdre is a tragic figure, she does not oppose or even disagree with her fate; consequently she does not have the emotional complexity of other Synge heroines.

Deirdre of the Sorrows is in many ways, therefore, an entirely new departure for Synge, and it seems that he wished it to be so. Nevertheless, Deirdre is yet another of those female protagonists whose restless spirits animate Synge's drama. It might be maintained that in her realization with Naisi of an ideal pastoral existence, in her being admired by all men for her beauty, and in her taking her own destiny in her hands by having the courage to oppose Conchubor and also to return to Ireland, she embodies the dreams of Nora Burke, Sarah Casey, Mary Doul, and Pegeen Mike. Indeed, one remembers Sarah Casey speaking of herself as the Beauty of Ballinacree by whom all men are attracted, Pegeen Mike rejecting her vow to Shawn to take the outlaw Playboy, Mary Doul dreaming of the awe her beauty arouses, and Nora Burke who was 'a hard child to please and a hard girl to please'. Whereas the earlier plays which feature the typical Synge heroine are all bitter comedies, *Deirdre of the Sorrows* is a tragedy in which a mood of resignation blurs and softens the savagery of the tale. Deirdre, unlike her sisters in drama, is not possessed by rage against mortality; she accepts that the price to be paid for youth's splendour is its passing, and she triumphs in evading the miseries of age, as the lovers in *Axel* triumphed by choosing to die at the height of the intensity of their dream. In this act of assertion, Deirdre, destroying herself, conquers the fates, just as Luasnad asserts his own individual life-force by a gesture of sexual passion at the point of his death, and as the Douls choose danger rather than ease in the service of their vision.

The setting of *Deirdre of the Sorrows* is not the springtime of *The Tinker's Wedding*; *Deirdre* is disturbed by no movements of May. The play opens in the autumn, when she gathers nuts in the woods, and the sons of Usna are out hunting. It is a time of harvest, of fruition, both for her girlhood and for the long-known prophecy. At twenty years old she is approaching what we now think of as her majority. The time for marriage and womanhood has come.

The first words of the play are ominous:

OLD WOMAN: She hasn't come yet is it, and it falling to the night.
LAVARCHAM: She has not. *Concealing her anxiety*. It's dark with the clouds are coming from the west and the south, but it isn't later than the common.
OLD WOMAN: It's later surely, and I hear tell the Sons of Usna, Naisi and his brothers, are above chasing hares for two days or three, and the same a while since when the moon was full. (IV. 183)

The moon is on the wane. The storm clouds are gathering. It is, we are later told, some time after Samhain. Deirdre has been growing 'wilfuller' for 'two months or three' (IV. 187). Though she knows of the prophecy, we are told that: 'It's not the dread of death or troubles that would tame her like' (IV. 189). Nor, it seems, is she to be tamed by earthly wealth, for she has hidden away all Conchubor's gifts and all the symbols of her status as his bride-to-be. On meeting her, Conchubor says:

The gods save you, Deirdre. I have come up bringing you rings and jewels from Emain Macha.
DEIRDRE: The gods save you.
CONCHUBOR: What have you brought from the hills?
DEIRDRE *quite self-possessed*: A bag of nuts, and twigs for our fires at the dawn of day.
CONCHUBOR *showing annoyance in spite of himself*: And it's that way you're picking up the manners will fit you to be Queen of Ulster?
DEIRDRE *made a little defiant by his tone*: I have no wish to be a queen.
(IV. 189–91)

Deirdre's wish is for:

a mate who'd be her likeness . . . a man with his hair like the raven maybe
and his skin like the snow and his lips like blood spilt on it.   (IV. 191)

Her description of her ideal mate is very much the traditional
one of folk-tale; indeed it is the very description used in some
versions of Snow-White and in other stories. By means of it we
are forced into realization that Deirdre thinks of her life not in
terms of 'political' reality, but in terms of the working out of an
ideal myth. It may be even that knowledge of the prophecy has
turned her mind to thinking of her life as a heroic drama; to
avoid or attempt to escape her fate would be to live her life on
a lesser plane than that possible to her. Certainly, having been
thrown into a panic by Conchubor's insistence on an early
marriage, she decides to enter gladly and heroically upon her
historic role and pulls out the rich clothes and tapestries and
furnishings:

I will dress like Emer in Dundealgan or Maeve in her house in Connaught.
If Conchubor'll make me a queen I'll have the right of a queen who is
master, taking her own choice and making a stir to the edges of the seas. . . .
                                                                    (IV. 199)

One is reminded of Sarah Casey saying:

It's at the dawn of day I do be thinking I'd have a right to be going off to the
rich tinkers do be travelling from Tibradden to the Tara Hill.   (IV. 9)

Deirdre is, however, not thinking of marriage with Conchubor,
but, like Sarah Casey, of the glory of her power over the hearts
of men, for she says:

And maybe from this day I will turn the men of Ireland like a wind blowing
on the heath.   (IV. 199)

When Naisi and his brothers enter they are ribald and lecherous.
Accused by Lavarcham of being a tippler and stealer, Naisi
says:

At your age you should know there are nights when a king like Conchubor
would spit upon his arm ring and queens will stick their tongues out at the
rising moon. We're that way this night, and it's not wine we're asking only.
. . . Where is the young girl told us we might shelter here?   (IV. 205)

Deirdre is not, however, to be mastered by the casual lust of

Naisi any more than by the wealth of Conchubor. When she reveals herself to Naisi in all her finery it is she and not he who is in control of the situation, and his lust is transformed into romantic love. At first, however, he resists her invitation, and tries to keep her at a distance. When she tells him:

... it's a sweet life you and I could have Naisi. ... It should be a sweet thing to have what is best and richest if it's for a short space only.   (IV. 209)

He replies, very distressed;

And we've a short space only to be triumphant and brave.   (IV. 209)

and later suggests:

Wouldn't we do well to wait, Deirdre, and I each twilight meeting you on the side of the hills?   (IV. 211)

Finally, however, he capitulates, and Deirdre, aware of the prophecy, is herself 'a little shaken by what has passed', knowing that she has chosen 'to destroy the world'. Ainnle marries the lovers with the words:

By the sun and moon and the whole earth, I wed Deirdre to Naisi. May the air bless you, and water and the wind, the sea, and all the hours of the sun and moon.   (IV. 215)

The first act thus shows Deirdre as the protagonist of the play, and as fully aware of the fate that lies in store. She has made her choice with a ruthless idealism that commands awe. This very fact makes some kinds of dramatic tension impossible. She alone of Synge's protagonists knows both her destiny and her symbolic significance. In this play the victims of the gods know they are victims from the very start and accept their roles. They are not, like Oedipus, ignorant of their sins, or, like Macbeth, deluded by a hope of escape from punishment. The interest of the play therefore now lies less in what happens, than in the attitudes of the characters towards the inevitable, and thus the drama becomes philosophical and psychological.

The second act is set in the early winter, seven years later. It begins with Lavarcham expressing a hope that Conchubor will allow them to return safely from exile, but Deirdre herself is fatalistic:

There's little power in oaths to stop what's coming, and little power in what I'd do Lavarcham, to change the story of Conchubor and Naisi and the things old men foretold. (IV. 217)

It is no use her making Naisi swear 'by the earth and the sun over it' (IV. 217) that he will not return to Emain in Conchubor's lifetime. Lavarcham may think somehow to alter destiny, but Deirdre cannot. She herself is prepared to go to Emain if Naisi so decides, and tells Lavarcham in a speech whose pessimism echoes the mood of many of Synge's mortality-haunted characters,

I've dread going or staying, Lavarcham. It's lonesome this place having happiness like ours till I'm asking each day, will this day match yesterday, and will tomorrow take a good place beside the same day in the year that's gone, and wondering all times is it a game worth playing, living on until you're dried and old, and our joy is gone forever. (IV. 219)

Lavarcham soon admits that her words of hope were without substance, and sees that 'the end is coming surely' (IV. 221).

Owen adds a very little harsh vitality to the play here with his coarser speech. Fergus tells Naisi:

You'd do well to come back to men and women are your match and comrades, and not be lingering until the day that you'll grow weary, and hurt Deirdre showing her the hardness in your eyes. . . . (IV. 227)

Finally Deirdre herself puts forward a similar argument:

NAISI: I've said we'd stay in Alban always?
DEIRDRE: There's no place to stay always. . . . It's a long time we've had, pressing the lips together, going up and down, resting in our arms, Naisi, waking with the smell of June in the tops of the grasses, and listening to the birds in the branches that are highest. . . . It's a long time we've had, but the end has come surely. (IV. 231)

A little later she says:

. . . isn't it a better thing to be following on to a near death, than to be bending the head down, and dragging with the feet, and seeing one day, a blight showing upon love where it is sweet and tender? (IV. 231–3)

Ainnle resists the decision to return, but is overborne. Deirdre again speaks of old age as misery, and adds:

. . . it's a lonesome thing to be away from Ireland always. (IV. 237)

The trouble with this act is that every speech of rebellion against the fates, though sometimes energetic, is half-hearted, and that every word of hope is immediately countered. The mood of Deirdre withstands in turn the rage of Lavarcham, the revelations of Owen, and the arguments of Ainnle, and all these attempts at escape appear futile even as they occur. Moreover, they seem curiously adventitious dramatically. The act is filled with meaningless action, unnecessary furor; the decision has been made and the mood set and there is no altering it.

The third act builds up some tension as Naisi, Deirdre and Lavarcham observe the succeeding signs of Conchubor's intent, but it cannot develop real tension as the mood of resignation has been far too firmly established in the previous act. The only interest can be in the manner in which the disaster takes place. Naisi is on the point of shaking hands with Conchubor when the sound of Ainnle and Ardan being killed is heard. Deirdre holds him from running to their help, and then, as he tells her roughly to let him go, she says:

Go to your brothers. . . . For seven years you have been kindly, but the hardness of death has come between us.

NAISI *looking at her aghast*: And you'll have me meet death with a hard word from your lips in my ear?

DEIRDRE: We've had a dream, but this night has waked us surely. In a little while we've lived too long, Naisi, and isn't it a poor thing we should miss the safety of the grave, and we trampling its edge?

AINNLE *behind*: Naisi, Naisi, we are attacked and ruined.

DEIRDRE: Let you go where they are calling! *She looks at him for an instant coldly.* Have you no shame loitering and talking and a cruel death facing Ainnle and Ardan in the woods?

NAISI *frantic*: They'll not get a death that's cruel and they with men alone. It's women that have loved are cruel only, and if I went on living from this day I'd be putting a curse on the lot of them I'd meet walking in the east or west, putting a curse on the sun that gave them beauty, and on the madder and the stone-crop put red upon their cloaks.

DEIRDRE *bitterly*: I'm well pleased there's no one this place to make a story that Naisi was a laughing-stock the night he died.

NAISI: There'd not be many'd make a story, for that mockery is in your eyes this night will spot the face of Emain with a plague of pitted graves.

He draws out his sword, throws down belt and cloak, and goes out.

CONCHUBOR *outside*: That is Naisi. Strike him.   (IV. 255-7)

The bitterness of Deirdre at sending Naisi to his death by her 'words without pity' is extreme, but it turns into self-pity almost immediately and she asks:

... who'll pity Deirdre has lost the lips of Naisi from her neck, and from her cheek forever: who'll pity Deirdre has lost the twilight in the woods with Naisi, when beech-trees were silver and copper, and ash-trees were fine gold?
(IV. 257–8)

The remainder of the play is filled with her lamentations. With an egotism that has been hers throughout, she stops Fergus and Conchubor threatening each other with the words:

Draw a little back with the squabbling of fools when I am broken up with misery. . . . I see the flames of Emain starting upward in the dark night, and because of me there will be weasels and wild cats crying on a lonely wall where there were queens and armies, and red gold, the way there will be a story told of a ruined city and a raving king and a woman will be young forever. . . . (IV. 267)

It is the answer to old Maurya's cry at the close of *Riders to the Sea*:

No man at all can be living for ever, and we must be satisfied. (III. 27)

It is the answer to time, to have created a story that will never be forgotten. Deirdre will escape old age. Just before she kills herself she says:

It's a pitiful thing, Conchubor, you have done this night in Emain, yet a thing will be a joy and triumph to [the] ends of life and time. (IV. 269)

The play as a whole has passages of great beauty and pathos, but after the first act it is dominated so much by the one mood that it has little dramatic tension. The lamentations of Deirdre at the end of the play are impressive, but repetitious. Indeed the number of speeches from the beginning of the second act to the end of the play in which she tells us that death is better than old age, and dying while young and in love is preferable to dying with cold emotions when age has chilled the heart, is considerable. There is irony in her sending Naisi to his death with that very coldness and scorn their early demise is supposed to enable them to avoid, but her bitterness at this is soon countered by a self-pity magnified into self-assertion by her heroic vision of herself. Her egotism is very marked throughout the play, and only shaken occasionally when she grows a little nervous at the events she herself is manipulating.

At the very end of the play Conchubor's treachery seems almost the direct outcome of Deirdre's death-wish, and one begins to pity his age and his confusion almost more than one pities Deirdre herself. For a few minutes, as he pleads with her to share 'a little peace' with him in Emain, and refers to his being 'old and lonesome' (IV. 259), he has our sympathy, if only because he is suffering that very condition which Deirdre herself has feared. Deirdre, however, shows no pity save for herself. She may be a heroic and magnificent creature, but she is finally a predator, a monster.

This is to put the case too strongly, but the overstatement points to an inadequacy at the heart of the play, in that we are at no point permitted to see Deirdre in terms other than her own, for all are captivated and blinded by her vision of herself. Other characters may from time to time attempt to interrupt the steady progress of her prophesied and accepted career, but the interruptions are futile and even Lavarcham, the most fully characterized of the other persons in the play, becomes little more than a stock figure required to introduce moments of false hope and inadequate criticism. Naisi is, after his first speech, a lay figure. Conchubor becomes an individual only for a moment at the close of the play. Synge was writing a play for Molly Allgood to star in, and he wrote her a 'star role', but in doing so crippled the whole work, and reduced its tension.

Synge suggested that it might be 'amusing' to compare his *Deirdre* with that of Yeats and AE. AE's *Deirdre* is not particularly successful, being rather weak in poetry and hardly more dramatic than Sir Samuel Ferguson's earlier and pedestrian attempt. Yeats' *Deirdre*, however, is another matter, and a comparison is not without interest.

Yeats introduces his one-act play by means of three musicians who act as chorus and bring the story up to the time of the return of Deirdre and Naoise from exile. They thus impress us with the legendary nature and heroic stature of the story up to this point and make it unnecessary for the characters themselves to boast of their importance. Fergus then enters and it is through his speeches, his doubts and confusions, that we approach the tragedy. He is, after all, convinced that Conchubar will keep his oath to spare the lovers. It is only after this that Deirdre and Naoise enter, and their conversation provides much ominous symbolism, but also an intelligible explanation of why they trusted Conchubar. Naoise says:

> Being High King, he cannot break his faith.
> I have his word and I must take that word,
> Or prove myself unworthy of my nurture
> Under a great man's roof.[19]

Fergus half remembers the prophecy but chooses to forget it. Deirdre talks to the musicians and hears 'terrible mysterious things' and wishes to run away, but Fergus and Naoise will have none of it. She is thus, unlike Synge's *Deirdre*, both the victim and the cause of the tragedy, and a complex and effective figure. Moreover, she agreed to go to Conchubar if he spares Naoise, and in a splendidly contrived scene, as she blames herself for her elopement and explains how admirable Naoise is, he is, behind her back, gagged and bound and taken away to be killed. It is this act of treachery that finally rouses her to dignity, as with both mockery and pride she challenges Conchubar to let her see Naoise's dead body. Her suicide takes place off stage. Conchubar is left with the last speech, in which Deirdre's stature is recognized most effectively because it is recognized by an enemy:

CONCHUBAR: You are all traitors, all against me – all. And she has deceived me a second time;
And every common man can keep his wife,
But not the King.
> *Loud shouting outside: 'Death to Conchubar!' 'Where is Naoise?' etc. The dark-faced men gather round Conchubar and draw their swords; but he motions them away.*
There's not a traitor that dare stop my way.
Howl, if you will; but I, being King, did right
In choosing her most fitting to be Queen,
And letting no boy lover take the sway.[20]

Yeats' Conchubar is a man whose decisiveness explains his

position. Synge's Conchubor has little dignity, is easily disturbed emotionally, and shows no capacities for leadership. Yeats' Deirdre is torn by several emotions, is confused and fearful as well as dignified and courageous. She is harrowed by the thoughts of what her beauty has done to men and even, at one point, threatens to mar it. She shows intelligence, even cunning, as well as passion. Synge's Deirdre is an egotistical young woman full of her own destiny and given to luxuriating in self-adoration, and self-pity. She is resigned to her fate from the start and, also, less forgivably, resigned to the fate of others. Yeats' suicide scene is restrained and dignified; his Deirdre shows wit in her final remark as she goes behind the curtain to kill herself upon Naoise's body.

> Now strike the wire, and sing to it a while,
> Knowing that all is happy, and that you know
> Within what bride-bed I shall lie this night,
> And by what man, and lie close up to him,
> For the bed's narrow, and there outsleep the cock-crow.[21]

It is the musicians who dignify Deirdre's death, but in a muted and restrained way. Fergus' comment on her death is even more tough and restrained:

> King, she is dead; but lay no hand upon her.
> What's this but empty cage and tangled wire,
> Now the bird's gone? But I'll not have you touch it.[22]

This contrasts with the self-dramatization of Synge's Deirdre and with the speech of Synge's Fergus:

Four white bodies are laid down together, four clear lights are quenched in Ireland. *He throws his sword into the grave.* . . . There is my sword that could not shield you, my four friends that were the dearest always. The flames of Emain have gone out: Deirdre is dead and there is none to keen her. That is the fate of Deirdre and Naisi next the Children of Usna and for this night Conchubor, our war is ended. (IV. 269)

Compared with the Yeats speech this is fustian. Moreover, here Synge exploits poetic imagery at the cost of sense. If Emain had started burning only a little while before, as appears to be the case, then the fires have burned out remarkably quickly. If there is none to keen Deirdre, what in heaven's name is Fergus doing? And what about Lavarcham? Synge has used his poetic licence too freely here.

The comparison that Synge suggested shows that Yeats wrote the better play; both the stage-craft and the characterization are superior. Moreover the language is clearer and stronger. There is no way out of it. Synge's incomplete *Deirdre of the Sorrows* is not that masterpiece he intended. It was generous of Yeats to say in introducing it to its first readers:

> ... it is probable he would have altered till the structure had become as strong and varied as in his other plays; and had he lived to do that, 'Deirdre of the Sorrows' would have been his masterwork, so much beauty is there in its course, and such wild nobleness in its end, and so poignant is an emotion and wisdom that were his own preparation for death. (IV. 179–80)

It is this last notion that must affect our attitude to *Deirdre of the Sorrows*. Synge was a sick and dying man as he laboured upon it, and was aware of the inevitability of his own death. It may be that for him it was not possible to create a mood of rebellion against the fates except in a brief burst of energy such as that shown in one of his last poems. He wrote a play in a new medium; he created a speech of great discipline and beauty; he presented in dramatic form a series of meditations upon approaching death. All these meditations, all these speeches, have power and beauty; they do not, however, add up to a play, but, as he himself suspected, to a narrative, a story for voices, a restatement of the views expressed so much more vividly and positively in earlier plays, that youth's splendour passes, that 'the heart's a wonder', and that what matters is not the small circumstances of our lives or deaths, but the way in which our vision can enhance the lives of others, giving them images of strength, courage, and beauty.

Deirdre of the Sorrows is poetic drama. It was written at a time when Synge was also turning to poetry again. He began to plan the play in 1906 and during the period 1906–8, while working on *Deirdre*, he revised many of his early poems and wrote a number of new ones. It is not completely successful as a play partly because the impulse towards lyrical statement is stronger than the impulse towards dramatic characterization. After the first act, it is basically a meditative monologue with interruptions. This monologue, however, not only restates views expressed in earlier works, but also, by abandoning a certain kind of irony, attempts to answer a question that is implied in all the plays and much of the prose. I have said that in Synge's drama the protagonists are unaware of the symbolic dignity of their own lives, and thus pursue lesser dignities than those they, in their own strong individualities, already possess. This suggests that one might ask what would happen if a character were absolutely and completely aware of his or her true dignity and of his or her fate. *Deirdre of the Sorrows* is aware both of her stature and her destiny. This knowledge, however, destroys her spiritually. It makes her prisoner of her own ego. It leads her to be both ruthless and self-centred. It turns her into a heroine who sees her life's only justification to be its tragic pattern, and the poetry of lamentation that can be made from it. Her values are the pure values of romance. She is possessed only by the impulse towards love and that towards death. She is forced by her belief in the prophecy to perfect her life in terms of these twin forces; she keeps love at its highest intensity and gives death its most heroic form.

This is epic material, and for it Synge constructed a language which he felt appropriate. Writing of Lady Gregory's *Cuchulain of Muirthemne* in *The Speaker* of 7 June 1902 in words I have already quoted, he said:

The Elizabethan vocabulary has a force and colour that make it the only form of English that is quite suitable for incidents of the epic kind, and in her intercourse with the peasants of the west Lady Gregory has learned to use this vocabulary in a new way, while she carries with her plaintive Gaelic constructions that make her language, in a true sense, a language of Ireland.

(II. 368)

In *Deirdre of the Sorrows* Synge himself attempted to present epic material in 'a true language of Ireland'. He failed, however, to realize that the values of the epic are so extreme, the egotism of the epic hero is so inhuman, and the quarrels and arguments of epic are so firmly based upon a system of values alien to our commonplace lives, that pure epic makes for poor drama. It must be adulterated, as Yeats realized, by touches of

150

the commonplace, by grossness, by humour even, otherwise drama becomes mere narrative, and dramatic tension is replaced by rhetoric. It is odd to reflect that Synge, as a lyric poet, understood what as a dramatic poet he failed apparently to perceive, though one must always remember that he himself knew *Deirdre of the Sorrows* to be unfinished and imperfect and felt it required strengthening. He was not given the time to strengthen it, and perhaps the whole play suffers from his being unable to avoid giving it an expression of his own resignation in the face of death and his own grief at the coming loss of that love which had during the years of its writing turned his mind again to romantic poetry. The *Deirdre* he created was created for Molly Allgood to play. It seems the blackest and most savage irony that she should be required doubly to lament the death of her lover, both in reality and upon the stage. Moreover, just as Deirdre, knowing her destiny, put an end to hope in Alban, in order to complete her tragic story, so J. M. Synge, knowing his destiny, postponed his marriage to Molly in order to complete his play. Synge's last play is, in some ways, as deeply personal a play as his first. In *When the Moon Has Set* and *Deirdre of the Sorrows* he took elements of his own life and suffering as material for his drama. In both plays he gave expression to his own fear of age and the dwindling away of life's splendour. His relationship with Molly was as unhallowed by Church and law as Deirdre's with Naisi. His love poems to Molly are often as pastoral as those Naisi might have written for Deirdre in Alban. Deirdre describes her ideal mate as 'a man with his hair like the raven maybe and his skin like the snow' (IV. 191), and Synge, writing to Molly, tells how their kisses are observed by 'a snowy gull and sooty daw' (I. 53). In a poem of 1906 he writes to Molly of how:

> Then in the hush of plots with shining trees
> We lay like Gods disguised in shabby dress,
> Making with birches, bracken, stars and seas,
> Green courts of pleasure for each long caress. (I. 43)

and the poem reminds one of Deirdre and Naisi in Alban. The connection between personal experience and this play could hardly fail to be close, for Molly had been thought of for the role of Deirdre from the very beginning. What is, however, disturbing, is that Synge appears to have created for his fiancée the role of a Muse figure who brings to her lover the three supreme gifts of poetry, love, and death.

It is not the business of this book to attempt to unravel this particular skein. It is, however, important to show that in his last play, as in his first, Synge was transfiguring actuality, and that all his plays, therefore, can be seen as deriving equally from personal experiences. Synge did not ever step far away from the life he knew. He saw it, from the beginning, in universal terms, and in his last play, he attempted to put upon the stage one of the most universal myths of all, that of the Belle Dame sans Merci, and fuse with it that of the Priestess destroyed by the furies of her own oracle.

CHAPTER TWELVE

The Poems

Synge's poems are few, and they do not have the thematic richness and profundity of his mature drama. Nevertheless they take up themes and attitudes which are present in his other work and tackle them from a different point of view, and his thoughts about poetry are as interesting and seminal as his thoughts on other matters.

When W. B. Yeats wrote, in a letter to his father, on 5 August 1913, 'There are always two types of poetry – Keats the type of vision, Burns a very obvious type of the other', he was repeating views he had read in a notebook of Synge's. This 1907 notebook, which Yeats saw when he went through Synge's papers after his death, makes the point at greater length. The passage runs:

Poetry roughly is of two kinds the poetry of real life – the Poetry of Burns, and Shakespeare, Villon, and the poetry of a land of the fancy – the poetry of Spenser and Keats and Ronsard. That is obvious enough, but what is highest in poetry is always reached where the dreamer is leaning out to reality or where the man of real life is lifted out of it.   (I. xiv–xv)

Synge made a similar point in a letter of 1908:

... if verse, even great verse is to be alive it must be occupied with the whole of life – as it was with Villon and Shakespeare's songs, and with Herrick and Burns. For although exalted verse is the highest, it cannot keep its power unless there is more essential vital verse at the side of it as ecclesiastical architecture cannot remain fine, when domestic architecture is debased.
     (I. xv–xvi)

These two passages seem to me to cast a good deal of light upon Synge's poetry, and upon his view of the poet's task. The first is from a rough draft of a possible preface to his poems, long before he finally decided to publish. The second is an extract from the letter he wrote to Yeats in September 1908, asking him for his opinion upon an enclosed group of poems. Yeats quotes his own version of this letter in his preface to Synge's *Poems and Translations*, and the difference between what Synge wrote and what Yeats *said* he wrote is extremely illuminating. The Yeats version of the above passage runs:

> ... if verse is to remain a living thing it must be occupied, when it likes, with the whole of a poet's life and experience as it was with Villon and Herrick and Burns; for though exalted verse may be the highest, it cannot keep its power unless there is more essentially vital verse – not necessarily written by the same man – at the side of it. (I. xxxi)

Synge's original letter also included the sentence, which Yeats entirely omits:

> Victor Hugo and Browning tried in a way to get life into verse but they were without humour which is the essentially poetic quality in what I call vital verse. (I. xvi)

It seems clear that Yeats was not only intent upon preventing Synge's memory being tarnished by the presentation of shaky critical judgments (Browning without humour, indeed!), but also concerned to clarify the meaning and limit the dogmatism of Synge's original. In doing this he changed the whole direction of the statement. The elements of Synge's attitude which he chose to suppress were, in fact, the most essential ones.

The notion of a poetry which is 'domestic' rather than 'ecclesiastical' which is 'vital' because of its 'humour', and which is 'occupied with the whole of life' is an important one in the history of English poetry. Synge chose Villon, Herrick, and Burns as illustrations, but he might equally well have picked on several members of the Tribe of Ben, and on the Cavaliers. It was the Cavalier poets' strength to make poetry look full of 'careless ease', to make it seem as if each poem were an impromptu, or, at the most, the work of an hour or two of pleasurable industry. The greater part of Carew's work looks as if, in the middle of a full life, he every now and again turned to poetry – for fun, or in a passing mood of affection or malice. Many of the poems refuse to take their own statements seriously;

pretentious sentiment may be presented, but it is liable to be mocked before the poem's end. Poetry is a by-product of living, and not a god in whose service life should be spent. The Cavalier poet is, essentially, a 'man of real life', who is occasionally 'lifted out of it' by some fantasy born of strong emotion or transfiguring thought.

If we think of Synge as a poet in this tradition, we can perhaps understand the force and significance of that word 'domestic'. The 'domestic architecture' is made to cope with the daily business of living; the 'ecclesiastical' is concerned to provide a place for exhortation, praise, and high sacrament. Poetry can involve itself in the daily business of living in two ways, either by observing it, or by becoming a part of it. Synge's poetry takes the latter course; it is used in the course of living, and in the furtherance of living. There are curses – poems which are constructed as if poetry could alter reality. There are inscriptions – poems made for the flyleaves of books and for tombstones, as if the poet really had a social function as a maker of sentences for special places and occasions. There are poems which are stray thoughts versified, spasms of the heart or intelligence. And there are several poems which tell an anecdote in the kind of language which presumes the existence of a listening audience. Synge, as a poet, succeeded in making for himself a persona which few poets have been able to imitate in the twentieth century. Perhaps only Yeats could make full use of it after Synge had died. It is this persona which is, to my mind, Synge's greatest contribution to the poetry of our time; it was also quite certainly an immensely formative influence upon the poetry made by Yeats after 1908.

It is not easy to define this persona accurately. It is partly that of the Cavalier, as I have described it. It is also, however, partly that of the poet who saw his vocation as a social function, and who had a strong sense of his role as orator. Synge may not, like Ben Jonson or John Skelton, run to making Masques. He may not produce elaborate complimentary poems, or appropriately orotund elegies. He does, however, in his balance of literary with vernacular diction, and in his counterpointing informal thought with formal manners of speech, continually remind us of the sense of genre which was once so important a part of a poet's equipment. His verse is usually written in the context of this understanding of genre; the success of his translations of Petrarch is, to a great extent, due to his setting a much simplified diction against a highly elaborate construction of thought; it is also due to his bland refusal ever to question or even indicate his premise that poetry of this kind is a natural rather than a falsely sophisticated activity. In the world in which Synge's poems are written it is still possible, if not to write a sonnet to my lady's eyebrow, to send her upon her birthday a verse which in all essentials could have been written in Elizabethan England, medieval Italy, or ancient Greece:

> Friend of Ronsard, Nashe and Beaumont,
> Lark of Ulster, Meath and Thomond,
> Heard from Smyrna and Sahara
> To the surf of Connemara,
> Lark of April, June, and May,
> Sing loudly this my Lady-day.   (I. 60)

Synge's own sense of tradition was as strong as his sense of mortality. Many of his poems are concerned with the passing of time, and with the inheritance of the past by the fleeting present. This is not very surprising in an Irishman, of course, for the habit of looking back upon legend and history was well established as a national literary characteristic before Synge came on the scene. Nevertheless, Synge's use of this theme is inimitable, and connects up directly with his view of the poet's task. A poem written at Coblenz goes:

> Oaks and beeches heath and rushes
> You've kept your graces by the Rhine
> Since Walter of the Vogelweide
> Sang from Coblenz to the Main
>
> But the great-great-great-great bastards
> Of the queens that Walter knew
> Wear pot-bellies in the breach
> And bald heads are potted too   (I. 61)

The tradition of singing is over. The glory has departed. It is an old and perpetually recurring cry, but Synge was before all else interested in those recurring cries of love or dread which each generation must make again. His deliberate renewal of tradition can be seen in the following poem which is so reminiscent of a well-known poem in Gaelic that one might even call it an 'imitation'.

> Some go to game, or pray in Rome
> I travel for my turning home
>
> For when I've been six months abroad
> Faith your kiss would brighten God! (I. 62)

The balance of passion and mortality in Synge's mature poems is almost Jacobean. Kiss and coffin are near neighbours. 'To the Oaks of Glencree' begins with an embrace and ends with the worms. 'In Kerry' places the wild, ecstatic, delight of the lovers alongside a stack of human bones. There is a continual resentment of the tricks of fate and the inevitability of death. The following quatrain could be the cry of any man against the President of the Immortals:

> You squirrel angel eel and bat
> You seal, sea-serpent water-hen
> You badger cur-dog mule and cat
> You player with the shapes of men (I. 65)

This anger finds expression over and over again in Synge's poetry, and while it must be seen as the expression of a deeply personal agony of mind, it must also be seen as a traditional cry, echoing down from whatever poet it was that first saw a life and feared for himself, and thought to curse the gods. Earlier in this book I quoted one example of Synge's use of this attitude. The poem was written in 1896–7.

> I curse my bearing, childhood, youth
> I curse the sea, sun, mountains, moon,
> I curse my learning, search for truth,
> I curse the dawning, night, and noon.
>
> Cold, joyless I will live, though clean,
> Nor, by my marriage, mould to earth
> Young lives to see what I have seen,
> To curse – as I have cursed – their birth. (I. 14)

This intemperate rage and despair is typical of Synge's early poems, in which (after an early attack of Wordsworthianism) he is clearly adopting a somewhat Byronic attitude. The verse is fevered, sub-hysterical. There are too many pieces of pretentious high-mindedness. Every now and then, however, the poems take on a knotted strength, a hardness of outline which Synge was usually able to seize upon and improve when he revised his early work. His revisions were almost always in the direction of making the poem more concrete in imagery and more brusque in statement. One poem of 1898 read originally as follows:

I waited and walked in the rue des Ecoles
And thought to see you arise from the West
And many a rake and rouged troll
Jeered my frozen zest

And when your hour was rung at the last
I stood with a shiver to watch the turn
And met two creaking coffins that past
Oh God! I am slow to learn.   (I. 21)

Synge's revisions of 1906–8 altered this to:

Rendez-vous manqué dans la rue Racine

When your hour was rung at last
I stood as in terror to watch and turn,
And met two creaking coffins that passed.
Lord God, I am slow to learn!   (I. 21)

Another instance of Synge's revision of early work is even more indicative of the way he regarded poetry at the end of his life. In 1907 he revised a poem of 1896 to read:

In the City Again

Wet winds and rain are in the street,
    Where I must pass alone,
Where no one wayfarer I meet
    That I have loved or known.

'Tis winter in my heart, the air
    Is willing, bitter cold,
While I am wailing with despair,
    As I have wailed of old.   (I. 16)

In the autumn of 1908 he tackled the poem again and produced:

Winter
With little money in a great city

There's snow in every street
Where I go up and down,
And there's no woman, man, or dog
That knows me in the town.

I know each shop, and all
These Jews and Russian Poles,
For I go walking night and noon
To spare my sack of coals.   (I. 63)

The significant change here is the movement from the general to the particular. The poem has become almost over-particular and limited by being so specific about the 'Jews and Russian Poles'. Others of Synge's mature poems have the same quality. 'The 'Mergency Man' refers specifically to 'Coom' and 'Coomasaharn'. 'Danny' is even more detailed geographically. 'In Kerry' refers to 'Thomas Flynn'. 'To the Oaks of Glencree' refers, not to some indefinite graveyard, but to 'Mount Jerome'. This deliberately narrowing use of detail is a part of the 'domestic' element in Synge's verse. The poems must be seen as being a part, not of any generalized life, but of a particular life in a particular place. One should be able to walk where the poem has been. It is one of poetry's tasks to show how the commonplace can be suddenly a miracle; to do that you need to identify the commonplace fairly precisely.

The interest in the passionate transfiguration of the commonplace led to Synge's balancing one kind of diction against another just as did his interest in tradition. In an unfinished poem of 1907–9 we find that while there is the expected use of 'romantic' language in such phrases as 'splendour of your eyes' and 'Stretched beneath a hazel bough', there is an unexpected use of detail in lines like 'Kissed from ear and throat to brow', 'Kissed from ear to ear', and 'Since your fingers, neck, and chin'. These are real, not fancy, kisses. The physical situation is clearly described *as* physical, even while it is being also attached to notions of paradisal splendour.

159

Is it a month since I and you
In the starlight of Glen Dubh
Stretched beneath a hazel bough
Kissed from ear and throat to brow,
Since your fingers, neck, and chin
Made the bars that fenced me in,
Till Paradise seemed but a wreck
Near your bosom, brow, and neck,
And stars grew wilder, growing wise,
In the splendour of your eyes!
Since the weasel wandered near
Whilst we kissed from ear to ear
And the wet and withered leaves
Blew about your cap and sleeves,
Till the moon sank tired through the ledge
Of the wet and windy hedge?
And we took the starry lane
Back to Dublin town again.   (I. 52)

This poem, perhaps because it was never really finished, shows the balance of explicit and implicit, factual and fanciful, simplicity and sophistication very clearly. It also hints at that use of hyperbole which Synge made his own, and which, lurking here behind the prison bars of the sixth line, emerges fully in 'In May'.

In a nook
That opened south,
You and I
Lay mouth to mouth.

A snowy gull
And sooty daw
Came and looked
With many a caw;

'Such,' I said,
'Are I and you,
When you've kissed me
Black and blue!'   (I. 53)

The absurdity, the wild fancifulness of the exaggeration qualifies the poem's whole tone, making it more affectionate, but also more passionate because less restrained verbally. This is the humour that gives vitality. We see it again in the 'stack of thigh-bones, jaws and shins' in the poem 'In Kerry' (I. 55), where the near-surrealistic image, however bitter, gives an air of almost savage exultation to the speaker's expression of joy. The perception of reality does not necessarily spoil the fantasy; it may enhance it.

> The chiffchaff and celandine
> The blackbird and the bee
> The chestnut branches topped with green
> Have met my love and me
> And we have played the masque of May
> So sweet and commonplace and gay   (I. 54)

It is commonplace but gay, and who cares if it is no more than a passing show? In Synge's poetry the cries of rage and despair must always be countered by expressions of gaiety, ecstasy even. In *The Death of Synge*, Yeats wrote: 'In Paris Synge once said to me, "We should unite stoicism, asceticism and ecstasy. Two of them have often come together, but the three never." ' Whether or not this statement is a reliable report of Synge's words, the feeling behind it is certainly one we find in these poems. Life and death, birth and decay are often in balance here. Synge's world is one where time is always nudging mankind. In the poem 'Samhain' we read:

> Though trees have many a flake
> Of copper, gold, and brass,
> And fields are in a lake
> Beneath the withered grass;
>
> Though hedges show their hips
> And leaves blow by the wall
> I taste upon your lips
> The whole year's festival.   (I. 42)

In his preface to his *Poems and Translations* Synge wrote:

In these days poetry is usually a flower of evil or good, but it is the timber of poetry that wears most surely, and there is no timber that has not strong roots among the clay and worms. Even if we grant that exalted poetry can be kept successful by itself, the strong things of life are needed in poetry also, to show that what is exalted, or tender, is not made by feeble blood. It may

almost be said that before verse can be human again it must learn to be
brutal. (I. xxxvi)

This has usually been taken as referring to such poems as 'The
'Mergency Man', 'Danny', and 'A Question' in particular,
and with some justice. These poems are more violent in expression than those of any other poet of the period save Masefield, though it was not until 1911, after Synge's death, that
he made use in 'The Everlasting Mercy' of that ultra-realistic
colloquialism for which he became famous. Synge first used
vulgar colloquialism in his poetry in 1895 when he wrote a
ballad in which a vagrant talks to a 'Horney' (policeman).
The policeman tells him that he would be wiser to steal something and go to prison where he would be taught a trade than
to go to the 'House' (i.e. the Workhouse or Union) to be a
'pauper'. The tramp calls the policeman a 'great dunder head',
and uses such colloquial phrases as 'hold your whist' and 'by
Jabs'. The poem is heavily ironic, but its vitality is beyond
question. It ends:

> By Jabs I niver had beleeved
> It was a Horney spoke
> Your comin nice and easy on
> Wid us young thinkin folk!
> Its deuced stiff a cove must steal
> To grow an honest man
> But Gob I'll do't if you think
> It is the best I can! (I. 9)

Synge took up the colloquial ballad again in 1907 when he
wrote 'Danny', based upon an anecdote he had heard in West
Kerry. It is relentlessly savage, and the climax is grotesque.

> Then Danny smashed the nose on Byrne,
> He split the lips on three,
> And bit across the right hand thumb
> Of one Red Shawn Magee.

> But seven tripped him up behind,
> And seven kicked before,
> And seven squeezed around his throat
> Till Danny kicked no more.

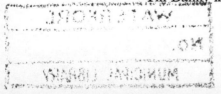

> Then some destroyed him with their heels,
> Some tramped him in the mud,
> Some stole his purse and timber pipe,
> And some washed off his blood.
>
> And when you're walking out the way
> From Bangor to Belmullet,
> You'll see a flat cross on a stone
> Where men choked Danny's gullet.

Not surprisingly, Elizabeth Yeats found this poem too strong for her stomach and apologetically excluded it from the Cuala Press edition of Synge's poems. She also excluded the equally forthright 'The Curse'.

Synge was doing more in 'Danny' than telling a crude story crudely. He was attempting to give a folk verse-form a content appropriate to the wild peasant folk he knew. He was implying, by this means, that most of the ballads of his day and even of earlier days, had got out of touch with the oral culture from which they originally sprang, and accusing them of a gentility wholly inappropriate to the genre.

'Danny' is the most violent of all Synge's colloquial poems, and the most obviously 'brutal'. It should not, however, be taken as illustrating all that Synge meant by the word 'brutal' in his preface. It is important to recognize that the violent juxtaposition of literary with colloquial language also has a brutal effect, and can be found in many poems. In point of fact, I'd suggest that the brutality Synge was after, though it finds one kind of expression in the ballads, is also clearly present in 'Queens' where the literary language does not so much counterpoint as come into a headlong clash with the vernacular. I would also suggest that the physicality of 'Samhain', or the poem beginning 'Is it a month', is another aspect of that brutality, that sense of the vigorously animal, which Synge felt to be as essential as humour to vital poetry.

'Queens' is, however, central to the understanding of Synge's poetry. It was worked out with immense care over many drafts, and the occasional apparently haphazard quality is the product of most careful craftsmanship.

163

Seven dog-days we let pass
Naming Queens in Glenmacnass,
All the rare and royal names
Wormy sheepskin yet retains,
Etain, Helen, Maeve, and Fand,
Golden Deirdre's tender hand,
Bert, the big-foot, sung by Villon,
Cassandra, Ronsard found in Lyon,
Queens of Sheba, Meath and Connaught,
Coifed with crown, or gaudy bonnet,
Queens whose finger once did stir men,
Queens were eaten of fleas and vermin. . . .   (I. 34)

The listing of great names in this manner is a habit of medieval poets rather than of modern ones. Moreover, the celebration of queens itself is somehow at odds with our century. The speaker of the poem, however, is looking back, not only upon the queens, but also, by implication, upon the days in which it was possible to list them and celebrate them with the appropriate high seriousness. Now, however, the list is bitter, crude, vulgarized; yet it still keeps 'in touch' with the old feeling of reverence, and partly by means of its own over-protestation of anti-romanticism. Thus in 'Queens' we get a curious fusion of the old with the new, of the professional Court-poet with the declassed functionless poet of today. It is a part of the poet's divine arrogance that he can still dare, in this twentieth century, to use and to abuse the old manner with the old confidence. As the Goliards implied reverence of the notions they caricatured so Synge suggests a persona by thus ostentatiously rejecting it, in this poem at any rate.

Reverence for the royal and legendary is as much part of the persona of Synge's poetry as is the rejection of the merely fanciful. The reverence is rather for great exemplars of human feeling, however, than for any notion of aristocracy. Synge could dismiss AE's mystical fairy-land as nonsense. He rejected the 'plumed yet skinny Shee' (I. 38). A 'man of real life', he was interested in celebrating the human vigour of the peasant in such poems as 'On an Island', 'Patch-Shaneen', 'Beg-Innish' and 'The 'Mergency Man'. His view of peasantry in these harshly gay-grim verses must have struck Yeats as a challenge, when he first read them in 1908. Yeats' own gentle picture of the haunted peasantry must have appeared odd beside Synge's, and the ballads of 'Patch-Shaneen', and 'Danny', must have seemed almost like criticisms of Yeats' own ballads of 'The Fiddler of Dooney', 'The Host of the Air', 'Father Gilligan', 'The Foxhunter' and 'Moll Magee'. The way in which several of Synge's poems treat of themes already treated by Yeats does look suspicious, certainly. 'On an Island' is, perhaps, the 'man of real life's' retort to the fanciful man's 'Lake Isle of Innisfree', and how many of Yeats' poems of sorrowing love can be considered answered by Synge's 'A Wish'? Here the lover's tears of frustration are regarded as a sauce for the dish. The poem suggests the speaker's agreement with John Donne that:

> Who ever loves, if he do not propose
> The right true end of love, he's one that goes
> To sea for nothing but to make him sick.

Synge, moreover, transfers the tears of frustration from the cheeks of the sighing lover to those of the beloved. Indeed, in the early version, sent to his fiancée, Molly Allgood, on 26 March 1907, the phrase 'well of pleasure' suggests that the beloved is sexually aroused. This version goes:

> May one sorrow every day
> Your festivity waylay.
> May seven tears in every week
> From your well of pleasure leak
> That I – signed with such a dew –
> May for my full pittance sue
> Of the Love forever curled
> Round the maypole of the world.
>
> Heavy riddles lie in this,
> Sorrow's sauce for every kiss.   (I. 51)

In the revised version published in 1909 the first lines read:

> May seven tears in every week
> Touch the hollow of your cheek,
> That I – signed with such a dew –
> For a lion's share may sue
> Of the roses ever curled
> Round the May-pole of the world.   (I. 51)

Synge indicates the riddling element of the poem explicitly enough for us to suppose him fully aware of the phallic and punning significance of the word 'maypole'. No one aware at all of the rose image in the early work of Yeats, and in much other work, could possibly avoid perceiving its sexual implications. The phrase 'lion's share' suggests something of the predatory, as well as implying (possibly) that there were other shares to be had. Indeed the poem-riddle suggests that the Beloved is not completely adorable, that she deserves to suffer somewhat for this particular lover, and that, far from being masochistically romantic, her man is inclined to relish her discomfort as being both an enhancement of his sense of conquest and a betrayal of weakness in the sex war.

If we turn from 'A Wish' to Yeats' love poems of this period, or to those about the 'Red Rose', we cannot help feeling that Synge had written his own poem in revolt against the conventional dreamy melancholies of the older poet. It seems not altogether impossible that Synge was himself keenly aware of this aspect of his work. He certainly did not let Yeats see his poems until George Roberts had already asked to publish them, and he showed John Masefield his ballad of 'Danny' over a year before he showed it to Yeats. Synge was a reticent man, but he worked in close harness with both Yeats and Lady Gregory; his silence about his poems must, surely, have been a conscious decision, even, perhaps, a strategy. Whatever the reason for Synge's not showing Yeats his verses until 1908 it is clear that once Yeats had read them he began to learn from them. It is extraordinary how much all the poems that Yeats had first printed after September 1908 and that appeared in *The Green Helmet* of 1910 differ from the poems printed before this date. Of the poems published in earlier collections only one or two have the faintest hint of that brusque hardness of tone which emerges so clearly in the 1910 collection. There are some poems in which the persona is that of the poet talking of himself as if his profession had social significance and an accepted stature, but these are almost apologetically couched in comparison with the 1910 verses in which this persona is used. Compare the poem 'Never give all the heart' and its use of both vocabulary and metre with 'At Galway Races'. The former was first printed in December 1905 and the latter in February 1909. The original version of the first began:

> Never give all the heart; for love
> Will hardly seem worth thinking of
> To passionate women, if it seem
> Certain and they never dream
> That it fades out from kiss to kiss,
> For everything that's lovely is
> But a brief dreamy kind delight . . .[23]

The original version of the second began:

> There where the racecourse is
> Delight makes all of the one mind
> The riders upon the swift horses
> The field that closes in behind.
> We too had good attendance once,
> Hearers, hearteners of the work,
> Aye, horsemen for companions
> Before the merchant and the clerk
> Breathed on the world with timid breath . . .[24]

The increase in gusto is formidable. The different view of the nature of delight is obvious. The imagery of the first could find a place in Pre-Raphaelite literature; the imagery of the second reminds me of nothing so much as of Jack B. Yeats' drawings in illustration of the race in *The Playboy of the Western World*. Of all the poems in *The Green Helmet* of 1910, only one was printed before September 1908. This is the first poem in the collection and differs from the remaining poems markedly, especially in its decorative prolixity in its first version, in which we read:

> There on the high and painted stern
> I held a painted steering oar
> And everywhere that I could turn
> Men ran upon the shore . . .[25]

It includes the word 'painted' again in the fifteenth line: 'And fish and crowd and painted ship'; and it ends with a, by now familiar, reference to 'the sweet name of Death'.

The 'sweetness' in the other poems in the collection is quite different:

> For she had fiery blood
> When I was young
> And trod so sweetly proud
> As t'were upon a cloud . . .
>
> *A Woman Homer Sung*[26]

> we that had thought
> To have lit upon as clean and sweet a tale
>
> *King and No King*[27]

> Such a delicate high head,
> All that sternness amid charm,
> All that sweetness amid strength . . .
>
> *Peace*[28]

The change is not, however, merely in a fresh perspective upon habitual epithets, a new muscularity and concreteness of imagery, a harsher use of the vernacular, but also in the presentation of a new version of the 'poet'. Pre-1910 Yeats could never have written:

> You say as I have often given tongue
> In praise of what another's said and sung
> 'Twere politic to do the like by these,
> But where's the wild dog that has praised his fleas?[29]

Originally grouped with several other poems under the general heading 'Momentary Thoughts', this quatrain was later given the even more significant heading 'To a Poet, who would have me praise certain bad poets, imitators of his and mine'. The persona of the professional poet, the poet who is at once the Court-poet and the Cavalier, the conscious craftsman and the impromptu wit, is emerging.

I do not wish to describe here the way in which this persona was exploited in Yeats' later work. I have done that elsewhere. It is easy enough, however, to notice its presence, and to claim the superb 'Under Ben Bulben' as a masterwork in the tradition. It is easy, too, to see how Yeats learned from Synge to balance kinds of diction against one another, so that many poems derive much of their excitement from the tension between pedantic and colloquial locutions. One might even maintain that the savage humour of Yeats' later short plays, as of some of his later poems, derives from his reading of Synge. An argument along these lines would be long and fruitless, for no one not already convinced of the truth of it could possibly be persuaded; the evidence in these matters is always wildly circumstantial and inconclusive. A careful reader might notice, with a smile, the number of words Yeats spent upon Synge as man, and as playwright, over the years, and the way in which he elevated him into his private pantheon of heroes. Such a reader might also notice that, at times, Yeats seems almost obsessed with the need to establish Synge's greatness; his claims on his behalf are those made for a prophet.

I would like to come out into the open here and admit that I am one who feels that Yeats owed more to Synge's poems than has ever been adequately recognized. I believe that he did not only learn a new forcefulness and clarity of diction, and a new way of balancing the literary against the colloquial, but also the use of a persona which he made central to his work as a lyric poet for the remainder of his life. I would add, also, that this persona provided by Synge was one which enabled Yeats to speak as a member of a long tradition of poets and scholars. He himself looked back at Goldsmith and Swift. Synge looked back to Herrick, Villon, Ronsard, Burns, and Petrarch. He might equally well have looked back to Ben Jonson, John Skelton, or, perhaps most of all, Dunbar, whose complaints, curses, and keenings have much in common with those in his own book, and who also knew how to balance the ornate against the vulgar, the literary against the colloquial. Moreover, Dunbar, like Synge, was 'occupied with the whole of life'. He, like Synge, was a 'man of real life' lifted out of it by passion and humour, just as Yeats learned to be a dreamer who leaned out to reality.

Perhaps the best comment upon Synge's poems, and upon the persona he rediscovered and renewed, with however careful a recognition of the way the mask must be worn, the strategy admitted, is one by Jack Yeats. In an essay 'With Synge in

Connemara', which was printed as a part of W. B. Yeats' Cuala Press volume *Synge and the Ireland of his Time* (1911), he wrote:

If he had lived in the days of piracy he would have been fiddler in a pirate-schooner, him they called 'the music' – 'The music' looked on at everything with dancing eyes but drew no sword, and when the schooner was taken and the pirates hung at Cape Corso Castle or the Island of Saint Christopher's 'the music' was spared because he *was* 'the music'.

This is the persona, all right. It has the ultimate gaiety described by Yeats in 'Lapis Lazuli':

> All things fall and are built again,
> And those that build them again are gay.[30]

Synge built again, and with that Yeatsian gaiety which can exist in the middle of despair and suffering. It is, perhaps, gaiety born of courage, of rebellion, of pride in the ability to face the real. In one of his very last poems Synge expressed in a fragment, most movingly, the rebellion that lies in the sense of mortality. In this poem he is both the representative of a tradition in which such poems are numerous, the representative of every man that faces death, and also his own most private, most local, most particular self. Person and persona are one; The voice, now fully achieved, ends in the middle of a task which Yeats was to take up and make into the greatest work of twentieth-century poetry.

> I read about the Blaskets and Dunquin,
> The Wicklow towns and fair days I've been in.
> I read of Galway, Mayo, Aranmore,
> And men with kelp along a wintry shore.
> Then I remembered that that 'I' and I,
> And I'd a filthy job – to waste and die. (I. 66)

Six months later he was dead, but he left behind him a couple of dozen poems that will always keep his name in mind as one of the great renewers of tradition.

CONCLUSION

It is impossible to sum up a man's world in a few pages, but perhaps I may end by allowing myself a few general observations which may link together some of the comments I have made earlier. It is my view that J. M. Synge was far from being the objective and sardonic observer of the Irish scene that some have thought him, and equally far from being the passionate devotee of all things simple and rural that others have supposed. He was a man who transformed every significant personal experience and encounter into literature, transfiguring all into fable with the energy of his imagination. He could not comfortably see the smallest evidence of human dignity, depravity, or passion without setting it in the context of the predicament of a human race granted both the potential of passionate life and the knowledge of ultimate death. He could not allow the existence of the commonplace, and though his natural bent was for bitter comedy, he saw the heroic in everything he met. Early troubled by the narrow savagery of the evangelical Protestant ethic and the blinkered complacency of Ascendancy bourgeois attitudes, he took up the cause of individual freedom and celebrated the anarchy of the passionate heart wherever he could find it. Disturbed by thoughts of his own mortality from an early age, he brought to his writings a vivid awareness of life's insecurity together with an intense relish for the gaiety and absurdity of its enjoyments, and created works whose richness and tension few have equalled. A passionate, but not a sentimental man, he strengthened the pathetic always with the grotesque or the harsh, and rather admired the splendour of

171

wholehearted grief than allowed himself to luxuriate in pity for it.

Synge was opposed to all easy solutions to complex problems. He found the 'wilful nationalism' of the patriots as offensive as the complacent conservatism of the Ascendancy. Himself inclined towards the mystical, he was suspicious of the dreamy vagueness of much romantic writing and challenged it in both prose and verse. While owing much to the encouragement and example of Yeats, he deliberately chose other and opposing tactics, even going so far as to exploit similar themes and materials in a different way. Though stubbornly opposed to softening his work in order to make it generally acceptable, he was extremely sensitive to criticism and, after the *Playboy* riots, chose to experiment with poetic and romantic drama rather than continue on his previous road. An innovator in the theatre, he based his innovations upon a strong belief in the significance of traditional elements in Irish culture, and upon his observation of the richness that came into being when old and new ways of life existed alongside each other. He was a highly conscious and deliberate writer, who took everything he wrote through numerous drafts, paying attention to every smallest detail. He was thrifty in that he threw very little away that might conceivably serve for future use; notes made in his twenties were pressed into service for works written in his middle thirties. Though he developed considerably over the years, the obsessions of his youth still operated during his maturity, and his earliest and latest writings have much in common; his vision is a unity from first to last. His influence upon later Irish and other writers has been immeasurable. The work of Sean O'Casey, George FitzMaurice, Jack Yeats, Samuel Beckett and a host of lesser writers owes an inestimable debt to Synge's discoveries. Perhaps one of his greatest debtors, however, was W. B. Yeats, to whom he himself owed so much, for it was Synge's poetry that taught Yeats to move ahead to his greatest work as a lyric poet, and was directly responsible for the shift in Yeats' style that occurred in the years 1908–10.

Synge does not fit easily into any of the pigeon-holes allotted him by his critics. Long regarded with Lady Gregory as the originator of a school of naturalistic peasant drama, he was, in fact, less concerned with naturalism than almost all his followers. Believed to be a simple, though eloquent, recorder of peasant life, he was, in truth, intent upon the creation of universal myth from particular experience. Dismissed for years as a poet of no importance, he wrote poems of an originality and strength far greater than those of many more lauded writers. His true qualities have been obscured from us by many accidents of history. Too many critics have, like Daniel Corkery, viewed his work only in relation to the nationalist movement of his time and to the theatrical revival of the Irish Renaissance. When these limitations upon one's vision are removed, it becomes clear that, while J. M. Synge was indeed passionately concerned with what was essentially Irish, and emotionally involved in working for the cultural renaissance of his country, his work is, in any serious sense of the word, international, for he tackled fundamental crises of the human spirit, and, in his shanachie plays especially, did not limit but extended the territory of twentieth-century drama.

SOURCE NOTES

1 David H. Greene and Edward M. Stephens, *J. M. Synge 1871–1909*, 1959, Collier-Macmillan, New York, 1961, p. 84.
2 Daniel Corkery, *Synge and Anglo-Irish Literature*, Cork University Press, 1931. Mercier Paperback, 1966, pp. 111–12.
3 Russell K. Alspach (Ed.), *The Variorum Edition of the Plays of W. B. Yeats*, Macmillan, 1966, p. 187.
4 *Ibid.*, p. 229.
5 Greene and Stephens, *op cit.*, p. 155.
6 Corkery, *op. cit.*, p. 152.
7 Peter Allt and Russell K. Alspach, *The Variorum Edition of the Poems of W. B. Yeats*, Macmillan Company, 1957, p. 757.
8 *Ibid.*, p. 764.
9 *Ibid.*, pp. 768–9.
10 Greene and Stephens, *op. cit.*, p. 140.
11 Robin Skelton and David R. Clark (Eds.), *Irish Renaissance*, Dolmen Press, Dublin, 1965, p. 72.
12 *Ibid.*, pp. 72–3.
13 Greene and Stephens, *op. cit.*, p. 71.
14 *Ibid.*, p. 243.
15 Skelton and Clark, *op. cit.*, p. 75.
16 Greene and Stephens, *op. cit.*, p. 249.
17 *Ibid.*, p. 257.
18 In Maurice Harmon (Ed.), *The Celtic Master, Being Contributions to the First James Joyce Symposium in Dublin*, Dolmen Press, Dublin, 1969, pp. 45–55. Stanley Sultan: A Joycean Look at The Playboy of the Western World.
19 Alspach, *op. cit.*, p. 355.
20 *Ibid.*, p. 388.
21 *Ibid.*, pp. 386–7.
22 *Ibid.*, p. 388.
23 Allt and Alspach, *op. cit.*, p. 202.
24 *Ibid.*, p. 266.

25 Peter Allt and Russell K. Alspach, *The Variorum Edition of the Poems of W. B. Yeats*, Macmillan Company, 1957, p. 253.

26 *Ibid.*, p. 255.

27 *Ibid.*, p. 258.

28 *Ibid.*, p. 259.

29 *Ibid.*, p. 262.

30 *Ibid.*, p. 566.

CHRONOLOGY AND BIBLIOGRAPHY

1871   16 April: John Millington Synge born in 2 Newtown Villas, Rathfarn-
        ham, near Dublin.

1872   J. M. Synge's father, John Hatch Synge, dies. Mrs Synge and her
        children, Robert, Annie, Edward, Samuel and John, move to 4
        Orwell Park, Rathgar.

1885?   Synge reads Darwin and suffers a crisis of faith.

1886   Joins the Dublin Naturalists' Field Club.

1887   Begins studying the violin with Patrick Griffith in Dublin.

1888   Enters Trinity College, Dublin.

1889   Attends lectures in Musical Theory at the Royal Academy of Music,
        Dublin.

1890   The Synge family moves to Crosthwaite Park, Kingstown (Dun
        Laoghaire).

1891   Synge joins the orchestra of the Royal Academy of Music and plays
        in the March concert.

1892   Awarded a scholarship in counterpoint by the Royal Academy of
        Music and receives a pass degree from Trinity College, Dublin. He
        falls in love with Cherry Matheson.

1893   Travels to Germany and studies music at Oberwerth, near Coblenz.
        POEM: 'Glencullen' in *Kottabos*, Hillary Term, p. 103.

1894   Travels to Würzburg to continue his music studies and, after spending the summer in Ireland, decides to give up music and go to Paris to study at the Sorbonne and teach English.

1895   Proposes to Cherry Matheson and is rejected. Begins writing *Vita Vecchia*. In Paris he studies socialism, attending lectures by the anarchist Sébastien Faure. He also renews his studies of Irish antiquities and the Irish Language. He meets Thérèse Beydon.

1896   Meets W. B. Yeats for the first time in Paris. Visits Italy where he meets Marie Antoinette Zdanowska and Hope Rea. He proposes formally to Cherry Matheson and is rejected.

1897   Joins the Irish League in January, but resigns from it in April. Begins to study mysticism and theosophy. A growth develops in his neck and his hair begins to fall out. He is operated on in the Mount Street Nursing Home, Dublin. He begins writing *Etude Morbide*.

1898   He returns to Paris in January, wearing a black wig. Attends Professor H. d'Arbois Jubainville's lectures on Celtic civilization and meets Margaret Hardon. On 10 May he arrives on Aranmor for the first time, and stays in the islands until 25 June, taking photographs and writing a journal of his experiences. He visits Lady Gregory at Coole Park, Co. Galway, and meets Edward Martyn. He proposes to Margaret Hardon and is rejected.
REVIEW: 'La Sagesse et la Destinée' (Maurice Maeterlink) in *The Daily Express* (Dublin), 17 December, p. 3.
ESSAY: *A Story from Inishmaan* in *The New Ireland Review* (Dublin) November, pp. 153–6.

1899   Visits Brittany and Aran for the second time, and completes *Etude Morbide*.
ESSAY: 'Anatole le Braz. A Breton Writer' in *The Daily Express*, (Dublin), 28 January, p. 3.

1900   Visits Aran for the third time and begins writing *When the Moon Has Set*, making use of much earlier notebook material.
REVIEW: 'The Poems of Geoffrey Keating' in *The Speaker* (London), 8 December, p. 245.
ESSAY: 'A Celtic Theatre' in *The Freeman's Journal* (Dublin), 22 March, p. 4.

1901   Visits Aran for the fourth time and completes *The Aran Islands*, which is rejected by Grant Richards at the end of the year. He completes a

two-act version of *When the Moon Has Set* which is rejected by Lady Gregory for the Irish Literary Theatre.
ESSAY: 'The Last Fortress of the Celt' in *The Gael* (New York), April 1901, p. 109.

1902   Writes *A Vernal Play, Luasnad, Capa and Laine, Riders to the Sea* and *In the Shadow of the Glen*, and begins *The Tinker's Wedding*. Fisher Unwin rejects *The Aran Islands*.
REVIEWS: 'An Epic of Ulster' (Lady Gregory: *Cuchulain of Muirthemne*) in *The Speaker* (London), 7 June, pp. 284–5.
'Irish Fairy Stories' (Seamus MacManus: *Donegal Fairy Stories*) in *The Speaker* (London), 21 June, p. 340. 'An Irish Historian' (Geoffrey Keating: *Foras Feasa Ar Eirinn: The History of Ireland*) in *The Speaker* (London), 6 September, pp. 505–6.
ESSAYS: 'La Vieille Litterature Irlandaise' in *L'Européen* (Paris), 15 March, p. 11.
'Le Mouvement Intellectual Irlandais' in *L'Européen* (Paris), 31 May, p. 12.
'The Old and New in Ireland' in *The Academy and Literature* (London), 6 September, pp. 238–9.

1903   Visits West Kerry for the first time. *Riders to the Sea* is rejected by *The Fortnightly*, but published in *Samhain*, 8 October. First performance of *In the Shadow of the Glen*. Begins writing *The Well of the Saints*.
REVIEW: 'Loti and Huysmans' (Pierre Loti: *L'Inde (sans les Anglais)*); Anatole France: *Monsieur Bergeret à Paris*; J. K. Huysmans: *L'Oblat*, in *The Speaker* (London), 18 April, pp. 57–8.
ESSAYS: 'A Dream on Inishmaan' in *The Green Sheaf* (London), Number 2, pp. 8–9.
'An Autumn Night in the Hills' in *The Gael* (New York), April, p. 117.
DRAMA: *Riders to the Sea* in *Samhain* (Dublin), October, pp. 25–33.

1904   Visits Mayo for the first time and revisits West Kerry. 25 February: First performance of *Riders to the Sea. Riders to the Sea* and *In the Shadow of the Glen* are performed in London at the Royalty Theatre. He completes the two-act version of *The Tinker's Wedding* and *The Well of the Saints*. Miss Horniman enters the scene and the Abbey Theatre is born.
REVIEWS: 'Celtic Mythology' (H. d'Arbois Jubainville: *The Irish Mythological Cycle and Celtic Mythology*) in *The Speaker* (London), 2 April, pp. 17–18.
'The Winged Destiny' (Fiona Macleod: *The Winged Destiny*) in *The Academy and Literature* (London), 12 November, p. 455.

DRAMA: *In the Shadow of the Glen* in *Samhain* (Dublin), December, pp. 34–44.
BOOK: *In the Shadow of the Glen* (John Quinn, New York). An edition of fifty copies.

1905   4 February: First performance of *The Well of the Saints*. Synge becomes a Director of the Irish National Theatre Society together with W. B. Yeats and Lady Gregory. Max Meyerfeld begins translating *The Well of the Saints* into German, and Pan Karel Musek starts translating *In the Shadow of the Glen* into Czech. In company with Jack B. Yeats Synge visits the 'Congested Districts' area of Mayo and Connemara in order to write articles about them for *The Manchester Guardian*. Molly Allgood joins the Abbey Theatre Company. Synge visits West Kerry for the third time.
ESSAYS: 'An Impression of Aran' in *The Manchester Guardian*, 24 January, p. 12.
'The Oppression of the Hills' in *The Manchester Guardian*, 15 February, p. 12.
'In the Congested Districts' in *The Manchester Guardian*, a series of twelve essays, with illustrations by Jack B. Yeats, published under the following titles and on the following dates: *From Galway to Gorumna*, 10 June; *Between the Bays of Carreroe*, 14 June; *Among the Relief Workers*, 17 June; *The Ferryman of Dinish Island*, 21 June; *The Kelp Makers*, 24 June; *The Boat Builders*, 28 June; *The Homes of the Harvestmen*, 1 July; *The Smaller Peasant Proprietors*, 5 July; *Erris*, 8 July; *The Inner Lands of Mayo*, 19 July; *The Small Town*, 22 July; *Possible Remedies*, 26 July.
BOOKS: *The Shadow of the Glen and Riders to the Sea* (Elkin Mathews, London).
The Well of the Saints (A. H. Bullen, London). *The Well of the Saints* (John Quinn, New York). An edition of fifty copies.
LETTER: To *The United Irishmen* (Dublin), concerning *In the Shadow of the Glen*. 11 February, p. 1.

1906   Synge falls in love with Molly Allgood and they become secretly engaged. He completes the first draft of *The Playboy of the Western World*, and accompanies the Abbey Theatre Company on tours of England, Ireland, and Scotland. Mrs Synge moves to Glendalough House, Glenageary, and he gives up his recently acquired flat in Rathgar and joins her there.
REVIEWS: 'A Translation of Irish Romance' (A. H. Leahy: *Heroic Romances of Ireland*) in *The Manchester Guardian*, 6 March, p. 5.
'The Fair Hills of Ireland' (Stephen Gwynn: *The Fair Hills of Ireland*) in *The Manchester Guardian*, 16 November, p. 5.

ESSAY: 'The Vagrants of Wicklow' in *The Shanachie* (Dublin), Autumn, pp. 93–8.

1907   26 January: First performance of *The Playboy of the Western World* causes riots in Dublin. It is performed with great success in Oxford and London. Synge is again operated on for a swelling in his neck. He begins writing *Deirdre of the Sorrows*. He suffers the first indications of a tumour in his side.
ESSAYS: 'At a Wicklow Fair' in *The Manchester Guardian*, 9 May, p. 12.
'The People of the Glens' in *The Shanachie* (Dublin), Spring, pp. 39–47.
'A Landlord's Garden in County Wicklow' in *The Manchester Guardian*, 1 July, p. 12.
'In West Kerry' in *The Shanachie* (Dublin), Summer, pp. 61–70.
'In West Kerry. The Blasket Islands' in *The Shanachie* (Dublin), Autumn, pp. 138–50.
In West Kerry. To Puck Fair'. in *The Shanachie* (Dublin). Winter, pp. 233–43.
LETTER: To *The Irish Times* concerning *The Playboy of the Western World*, 31 January.
BOOKS: *The Playboy of the Western World* (Maunsel & Co., Dublin). Issued at first in paper as Volume X of the Abbey Theatre series, and then in boards with a Preface by Synge.
The Aran Islands (Elkin Mathews, London, and Maunsel & Co., Dublin). Issued in both an ordinary and a large-paper edition, each with illustrations by Jack B. Yeats. The large-paper version was signed by author and illustrator. Some copies of the ordinary edition carry the date 1906.

1908   Exploratory surgery reveals that the growth in Synge's side is inoperable. He continues working on *Deirdre of the Sorrows* and postpones his marriage plans. During his autumn visit to Oberwerth his mother dies. His poems are accepted for publication, first in a small edition from the Cuala Press and then in a larger trade edition from Maunsel & Co.
ESSAYS: 'Good Pictures in Dublin. The New Municipal Gallery' in *The Manchester Guardian*, 24 January, p. 12.
'In Wicklow. On the Road.' in *The Manchester Guardian*, 10 December, p. 14.
BOOK: *The Tinker's Wedding* (Maunsel & Co., Dublin).

1909   24 March: John Millington Synge dies of Hodgkin's Disease in the Elpis Nursing Home, Dublin.

POSTHUMOUS FIRST PERFORMANCES AND SIGNIFICANT PUBLICATIONS

1909   11 November: First performance of *The Tinker's Wedding* at His Majesty's Theatre, London, by the Afternoon Theatre Company.
J. M. Synge. *Poems and Translations* (Cuala Press, Churchtown, Dublin. An edition of 250 copies.
J. M. Synge. *Poems and Translations* (John Quinn, New York). An edition of fifty copies.

1910   13 January: First performance of *Deirdre of the Sorrows* under the direction of Maire O'Neill (Molly Allgood), who played Deirdre.
J. M. Synge. *Deirdre of the Sorrows* (Cuala Press, Churchtown, Dublin). An edition of 250 copies.
J. M. Synge. *Deirdre of the Sorrows* (John Quinn, New York). An edition of fifty copies, some of which were destroyed and some reissued with nine pages of errata.
The Works of John M. Synge (Maunsel & Co., Dublin):
Volume I: *The Shadow of the Glen, Riders to the Sea, The Tinker's Wedding, The Well of the Saints.*
Volume II: *The Playboy of the Western World, Deirdre of the Sorrows, Poems, Translations from Petrarch, Translations from Villon and others.*
Volume III: *The Aran Islands.*
Volume IV: *In Wicklow, In West Kerry, In the Congested Districts, Under Ether.*

1911   W. B. Yeats. *Synge and the Ireland of his Time* (Cuala Press, Dundrum, Dublin). This contains an essay by Jack B. Yeats, *With Synge in Connemara*. An edition of 350 copies.

1912   Francis J. Bickley. *J. M. Synge and the Irish Dramatic Movement* (Constable, London).
P. P. Howe. *J. M. Synge: A Critical Study* (Secker, London).

1913   Lady Augusta Gregory. *Our Irish Theatre* (Putnams, New York).
Maurice Bourgeois. *John Millington Synge and the Irish Theatre* (Constable, London).

1915   John Masefield. *John M. Synge: A Few Personal Recollections with Biographical Notes* (Cuala Press, Dublin). An edition of 350 copies.

1918   Ernest A. Boyd. *The Contemporary Drama of Ireland* (Talbot Press, Dublin).

1931   Rev. Samuel Synge. *Letters to My Daughter: Memories of John Millington Synge* (Talbot Press, Dublin).
Daniel Corkery. *Synge and Anglo-Irish Literature* (Cork University Press).

1932   *Plays by John M. Synge* (Allen & Unwin, London). This edition contains some previously unpublished material.

1935   W. G. Fay and Catherine Carswell. *The Fays of the Abbey Theatre* (Rich and Cowan, London).

1939   Una Ellis-Fermor. *The Irish Dramatic Movement* (Methuen, London).

1941   L. A. G. Strong. *John Millington Synge* (Allen & Unwin, London).

1950   Peter Kavanagh. *The Story of the Abbey Theatre* (Devin-Adair, New York).

1951   Lennox Robinson. *Ireland's Abbey Theatre* (Sidgwick & Jackson, London).

1958   Gerard Fay. *The Abbey Theatre: Cradle of Genius* (Clonmore & Reynolds, Dublin).

1959   David H. Greene and Edward M. Stephens. *J. M. Synge 1871–1909*, Collier-Macmillan, New York). The authorized biography, which includes much previously unpublished material by J. M. Synge.
Mary Pollard and Ian MacPhail. *John Millington Synge (1871–1909): A Catalogue of an Exhibition held at Trinity College Library, Dublin, on the Occasion of the Fiftieth Anniversary of his Death.* (For the friends of the Library of Trinity College. This is the most reliable bibliography so far published. It should be read in conjunction with an article by Ian MacPhail in *The Irish Book* for Spring 1959.
Lawrence Wilson (Ed.): *J. M. Synge: Some Letters and Documents* (printed for the editor). An edition of 250 copies.
Ann Saddlemyer (Ed.). 'Synge to MacKenna: The Mature Years' in Robin Skelton and David R. Clark (Eds.): *Irish Renaissance* (Dolmen Press, Dublin).

1961   Robin Skelton (Ed.): *J. M. Synge: Translations* (Dolmen Press, Dublin). An edition of 750 copies.
Alan Price. *Synge and Anglo-Irish Drama* (Methuen, London).

1962   Robin Skelton (Ed.): *J. M. Synge: Collected Works. Volume I. Poems* (Oxford University Press, London and New York). Contains much previously unpublished material.

1965   Ann Saddlemyer. 'A Share in the Dignity of the World; J. M. Synge's Aesthetic Theory' in Robin Skelton and Ann Saddlemyer (Eds.): *The World of W. B. Yeats* (Dolmen Press, Dublin, and Washington University Press, Seattle, USA).

1966   Alan Price (Ed.): *J. M. Synge: Collected Works. Volume II. Prose* (Oxford University Press, London and New York). Contains much previously unpublished material.

1968   Ann Saddlemyer (Ed.): *J. M. Synge: Collected Works. Volume III. Plays* (Oxford University Press, London and New York).
Ann Saddlemyer (Ed.): *J. M. Synge: Collected Works. Volume IV. Plays* (Oxford University Press, London and New York). These volumes contain much previously unpublished material, including the verse drama and *When the Moon Has Set*.
Ann Saddlemyer. *J. M. Synge and Modern Comedy* (Dolmen Press, Dublin).

1969   Robin Skelton (Ed.): *Riders to the Sea* (Dolmen Press, Dublin). An edition of the Houghton Library typescript of the play. The prefatory material contains some details of the play's publication history which are not to be found elsewhere. An edition of 750 copies.
Stanley Sultan. 'A Joycean Look at the Playboy of the Western World' in Maurice Harmon (Ed.): *The Celtic Master, Being Contributions to the First James Joyce Symposium in Dublin* (Dolmen Press, Dublin).

1971   Robin Skelton. *J. M. Synge and His World* (Thames and Hudson, London).
Robin Skelton. *Synge Petrach* (Dolmen Press, Dublin).
Ann Saddlemyer (Ed.). Letters to Molly: *John M. Synge to Maire O'Neill* (Harvard University Press).
Ann Saddlemyer (Ed.). *J. M. Synge to Lady Gregory and W. B. Yeats* (Cuala Press, Dublin).
Ann Saddlemyer (Ed). *Theatre Business, Management of Men. The Letters of the First Abbey Theatre Directors* (New York Public Library).

INDEX

ABBEY THEATRE, Dublin, 17, 66; production of *Deirdre of the Sorrows* at, 132; first performance of *The Well of the Saints* at, 92
'About Literature' in *Collected Works of J. M. Synge* (Prose, ed. Price), 103
The Academy and Literature, 107
AE, *see* Russell, George W.
Afternoon Theatre Company, 79
Allgood, Molly (Maire O'Neill), 132, 139, 146, 151–2, 165
America, English language in, 107; Irish emigration to, 105, 106; *Playboy* rows in, 115
ancient beliefs and stories, 31–2, 33, 38, 74; culture and wisdom, 14, 35, 111, 112, 113
anti-clericalism, 15, 22, 65, 70, 76, 78; *see also* Christianity
antiquarians, 29, 30–1
Aran cases, 115
Aran Islands, islanders, 'aristocratic' feeling of, 36, 38; awareness of isolation and mortality, 33–4, 38; cultural inheritance of, 30–2, 38, 40; and natural moral sense, 37–8; primitive sensibility of, 27, 38; Rev. Alexander Synge's missionary work on, 25–7; Synge's myth-making interpretation of, 35, 37, 38, 39–40; W. B. Yeats advises Synge to go to, 24, 39
The Aran Islands (Synge), 14, 15, 16, 20, 24–40, 41, 45, 46–7, 53, 64, 91, 103, 108, 122, 123; 'Ballad of the White Horse' in, 32; 'Phelim and

the Eagle' in, 33; 'Rucard Mor' in, 32
aristocracy, Aran Islander's feeling of, 36, 38; Synge's nostalgia for vanishing, 109–10
art, artistic creation, 15; national element in, 66–7; 'personal', 20–1; Synge's views on, 103, 113
Ascendancy bourgeois attitudes, 171, 172
Au Pays des Pardons (le Braz), 25
autobiographical notes, 9–10, 12, 18, 22, 103
Axel, 140

BAUDELAIRE, CHARLES, 15
Beckett, Samuel, 172
'black birds', mythological significance of, 45–6, 47
Blake, William, 36
Boccaccio, Giovanni, 55, 66, 79
Braz, Anatole le, 25, 39, 79
Brittany, 14, 25, 32
Brodney, Spenser, 28
Brodsky, Leon, 17
Browning, Robert, 154
Burns, Robert, 153, 154, 169
Byron, Lord George Gordon, 86

CAIN (Byron), 86
Carew, Thomas, 154
Cathleen ni Houlihan (Yeats), 42, 51, 54
Cavalier poets, 154–5
Celtic culture, legends, 13, 25, 48, 66
The Celtic Twilight (Yeats), 25, 40
Cervantes, Miguel, 117